THIS IS LOVE, NOT RELIGION

How to Be Strengthened by Boundaries,
Abide in Identity, and Live in Purpose

AIDEN SAUNDERS

This Is Love, Not Religion

How to Be Strengthened by Boundaries, Abide in Identity, and Live in Purpose

By Aiden Saunders

How to Be Strengthened by Boundaries, Abide in Identity, and Live in Purpose

Copyright © 2025 Aiden Saunders

All rights reserved solely by the author. The author guarantees all contents are original and do not infringe upon the rights of any other person or work. No part of this book may be reproduced or transmitted in any form or by any means without prior written permission of the author.

Unless otherwise indicated:

Scripture quotations marked NIV are taken from The Holy Bible, New International Version. Copyright © 1973, 1978, 1984 by Biblica, Inc.™ Used by permission. All rights reserved worldwide.

Scripture quotations marked KJV are taken from The Holy Bible, King James Version. Public domain.

Artwork credit: Certain artwork used in this book was created by Kaydene Parker and is used with permission. All rights remain with the artist.

ISBN: 978-1-9160929-2-1

Published by D.O.V Publishing House

Printed in the United Kingdom.

This Is Love, Not Religion

This book was inspired by: Jesus Christ, His church, teachers, family, and friends.

Thank you.

How to Be Strengthened by Boundaries, Abide in Identity, and Live in Purpose

Contents

How the Book Is Organised...10
    Part I: The Vine – Living from the Inside Out.............................10
    Part II: The Fruit – Living a Life That Reveals Heaven...............11
    How to Use This Book..12

Introduction - Part I: When the Seed Breaks Open................................ 13
    I. A Seed Must First Fall...13
    II. An Invitation to Grow... 14
    III. What Sets This Journey Apart... 14

Introduction - Part II: The Framework of Growth..............................16
    I. The Framework: Roots → Vine → Fruits → Seasons............... 16
    II. A Bridge of Spirit-Filled Fruit..22
    III. The Method: How This Book Will Aid Your Transformation......... 22
    IV. The Journey Begins... 24
    A Prayer Before You Begin... 24

Part I.. 25

Chapter 1: Boundaries - Guardrails of Growth...................................26
    What Are Boundaries?..26
    The Rooted Spirit Manifested: The Spirit of the Fear of the Lord....28
    Creation and the First Boundary.. 29
    A Living Example: Moses Withdraws (Exodus 2)......................31
    The Scenario: A Life Without Lines... 32
    My Turning Point: The Birthing Of Freedom............................. 34
    Practicing Boundaries in Real Life... 43
    Closing Thoughts...50

Chapter 2: Identity - Becoming Who We Really Are.........................54
    What Is Identity?..54
    The Rooted Spirit Manifested: The Spirit of Knowledge.........57
    Creation and the Formation of Identity......................................62
    A Living Example: Moses Wrestles with Who He Is (Exodus 3–4)...65
    The Scenario: The Unsettled Soul.. 68
    My Turning Point: The Surrendering Of Self............................. 69
    Practicing Identity in Real Life.. 76
    Closing Thoughts.. 84

Chapter 3: Animation - Expressing Our True Self.............................89
    What Is Animation?..89

The Rooted Spirit Manifested: The Spirit of Counsel............................91
Creation and the Third Day..93
A Living Example: Moses Finds His Voice (Exodus 3–4)..................94
The Scenario: When Identity Waits in Silence....................................96
My Turning Point: The Release in Lockdown....................................97
Practicing Animation in Real Life..99
Closing Thoughts..112

Chapter 4: Management - Bringing Order from Chaos............117
What Is Management?..117
The Rooted Spirit Manifested: The Spirit of Understanding............119
Creation and the Fourth Day...120
A Living Example: Moses organises the People (Exodus 18)...........124
The Scenario: When Passion Turns to Pressure...............................126
My Turning Point: Learning to Tend What God Gave Me...............128
Practicing Management in Daily Life..140
Closing Thoughts..145

Chapter 5: Artistry - Creating from the Inside Out....................150
What Is Artistry?...150
The Rooted Spirit Manifested: The Spirit of Wisdom......................152
Creation and the Fifth Day...154
A Living Example: Moses the Visionary Builder (Exodus 25–31)...158
The Scenario: When Creativity Lacks Flow......................................160
My Turning Point: Learning to Create with Wisdom.......................160
Practicing Artistry in Daily Life: The S.O.W. Rhythm....................168
Closing Thoughts..172

Chapter 6: Purpose - Walking in Your Divine Design................176
What Is Purpose?..176
The Rooted Spirit Manifested: The Spirit of Might.........................180
Creation and the Sixth Day..181
A Living Example: Moses at the Red Sea (Exodus 14)....................185
The Scenario: The Vision with No Fuel..186
My Turning Point: The Yielded Trust...187
Practicing Purpose in Daily Life..195
Closing Thoughts..198

Chapter 7: Love - The Crown That Holds It All.........................203
What Is Love?..203
The Rooted Spirit Manifested: The Spirit of the Lord.....................208
Creation and the Seventh Day...211
A Living Example: Moses Asks for Presence (Exodus 33)...............212

How to Be Strengthened by Boundaries, Abide in Identity, and Live in Purpose

- The Scenario: When You Love but Feel Empty..................................214
- My Turning Point: The Freedom of Being..................................216
- Practicing Love in Daily Life..................................220
- Closing Thoughts..................................228

Part II..................................233

Chapter 8: Fruitfulness - Experiencing Growth..................................234
- The Garden of Becoming..................................234
- The Fruit of the Spirit: What God Grows in You..................................236
- Not All Fruit Is Healthy Fruit..................................241
- The Fruits of Life: Where Heaven Touches Earth..................................242
- Living the Fruits..................................253
- The Battle for Inner Ground..................................253
- Tending the Garden: Fruitfulness as a Lifestyle..................................255
- Closing Thoughts..................................259

Chapter 9: The Seasons - Embracing The Rhythm for Growth..................263
- The Wisdom of Seasons..................................263
- The Four Seasons of Growth..................................264
- The Fruits Flow Through Seasons..................................264
- Your Personal Season..................................267
- The Spiral of Spiritual Growth..................................267
- Practicing Seasonal Awareness..................................269
- Closing Thoughts..................................270

Chapter 10: Becoming in the Kingdom of Light..................................273
- Kingdom Culture: The Boundaries That Protect What's Pure.......273
- The Beatitudes: Becoming a Light in the Kingdom..................278
- Light That Cannot Be Hidden..................................284
- Prayer of Becoming: Form Me by the Beatitudes..................285

Chapter 11: The Kingdom Invitation: Coming to Christ, Dying to Self, and Rising in New Life..................................288
- Why Jesus Had to Die—and Rise Again..................................290
- The Gospel of the Kingdom of God..................................291
- Receiving the Holy Spirit: The Return of Divine Breath...................295
- What You Must Do..................................295
- Baptism: The Death that Brings Life..................................296
- The Burning Bush, the Living Branches, and the Eternal Flame. 298
- A Sacred Pause: Yielding to Christ..................................298
- A Prayer of Salvation..................................299

Final Thoughts: Rooted for Life – Becoming the Tree We Were Born to

This Is Love, Not Religion

Be 300
    You Are Becoming the Tree 301
    An Invitation to Remain 302
    Have Grace for One Another 302
    Love and the Will: Stones in the Wilderness 304
    The Bigger Picture 311
    A Final Blessing 312

About the Author 315

How to Be Strengthened by Boundaries, Abide in Identity, and Live in Purpose

*"I am the true vine, and my Father is the gardener.
He cuts off every branch in me that bears no fruit,
while every branch that does bear fruit he prunes so that it will be even more fruitful.
You are already clean because of the word I have spoken to you.
Remain in me, as I also remain in you.
No branch can bear fruit by itself; it must remain in the vine.
Neither can you bear fruit unless you remain in me.
I am the vine; you are the branches.
If you remain in me and I in you, you will bear much fruit;
apart from me you can do nothing."
(John 15:1–5, NIV)*

How the Book Is Organised

This book is a journey in two parts,
from the roots within to the fruit that flows.

Each part reveals a distinct layer of transformation,
Yet both are connected by one truth:
You cannot grow what you do not first become.

Part I: The Vine – Living from the Inside Out

The first part of this book is about abiding, the sacred, inner formation that happens when you align with the life of Christ.

These seven chapters explore what it means to be rooted in Him through the Vine.
Each one represents a pillar of growth that shapes your identity and strengthens your foundation.

- **Boundaries**: Guardrails of growth
- **Identity**: Becoming who you really are
- **Animation**: Expressing your true self
- **Management**: Bringing order from chaos
- **Artistry**: Creating from the inside out
- **Purpose**: Walking in your divine design
- **Love**: The crown that holds it all

This part will guide you in discovering the Spirit within, the Vine that gives life to everything else.

How the Book Is Organised

Part II: The Fruit – Living a Life That Reveals Heaven

The second part is about becoming,
The outward evidence of your inner alignment.

This is where the life formed in the Vine becomes visible in the world.
You'll explore the Fruit of the Spirit, the rhythms of spiritual seasons, and the way God's Kingdom flows through you.

- **Fruitfulness**: Experiencing growth
- **Season**: Embracing the rhythm for growth
- **Becoming in the Kingdom of Light**: Living in your renewed nature
- **The Kingdom Invitation**: Extending what you've received
- **Final Thoughts**: Rooted for life

This fruit section helps you see how love matures into action,
How presence becomes practice,
And how your life becomes a witness of what it's rooted in.

Each section builds upon the last:
From foundation, to formation, to fruitfulness.

This is not just a book to read.
It offers a pattern to live by.
A rhythm to return to.

And as you walk through it, you'll discover:
You weren't just made to believe.
You were made to become.

How to Use This Book

This is not a book to rush through. You may want to read it chapter by chapter, reflecting slowly as you go. Some sections might speak louder in certain seasons of life. Return to them when needed.

Let the process be sacred, not rushed.
This book's aim is to help you flow in rest,
A sabbath in Christ,
So that you can focus on dressing and keeping your garden.

You'll notice that parts of this book carry a different style and cadence than a traditional read. That's intentional.
Some lines are written in rhythm,
Meant to be felt, not just read.
They're designed to slow you down, so the truths can sink in deeper.

You can:
- Journal after each chapter using the prompts provided.
- Sit with the Scriptures, letting them shape your thinking.
- Share reflections with a friend or group.

It's designed to be lived with, not just read through.

Introduction - Part I: When the Seed Breaks Open

How Brokenness Becomes the Soil for Growth

"Very truly I tell you, unless a kernel of wheat falls to the ground and dies, it remains only a single seed. But if it dies, it produces many seeds."
(John 12:24, NIV)

I. A Seed Must First Fall

There was a season when I didn't know who I was anymore.

On the outside, I kept going, working, smiling, surviving. But inside, I felt like a wintered tree: stripped bare, weary, and uncertain if I'd ever feel truly alive again. Dreams that once stirred me had gone quiet. My faith felt like whispers in the dark. The soil of my life seemed barren.

That season wasn't the end; it was the sacred beginning of something new.

Looking back, I see that the struggle wasn't punishment, it was planting. The darkness wasn't my downfall, it was the soil. What I thought was falling apart was really the moment a seed breaks open… so life can begin.

That seed became this book. And now, this book will hopefully become a seed for you.

II. An Invitation to Grow

Whether you're thriving or barely holding on,
Rooted in Christ (anchored in relationship with Jesus) or carrying different beliefs,
This journey is for you.

You don't need all the answers to begin.
Some of the most life-changing journeys
Start not with certainty, but with hunger.
What matters most is your willingness to grow.

III. What Sets This Journey Apart

This book isn't about striving harder
Or pretending everything is fine.
It's about slowing down,
For as long as you need to,
In order to root yourself in what is real.

It's about growing deep before you grow wide.
It's about discovering that the life you long for
Isn't out there somewhere,
It's already within, waiting to root and bloom.

While this book is rooted in my Christian faith,
It speaks to all people.

The principles and framework shared here,
Shaped through personal experience, spiritual insight (often called revelation), Scripture, and my coaching practice,
Are designed to meet you where you are.

Whether you're a believer, seeker, or simply curious,
These concepts offer practical guidance
For anyone pursuing growth, purpose, and wholeness.

Introduction - Part I: When the Seed Breaks Open

This is not just theory. It's the fruit of what I've lived, taught, and witnessed as a Follower of Christ and a life coach (Personal Growth Partner).

My hope is that through this journey,
You'll cultivate deeper self-awareness,
Greater alignment,
And a life that bears fruit,
In every area that matters.

You are welcome here.

If you're willing to pause, reflect, and open your heart,
You'll find wisdom here that doesn't demand perfection,
Only presence.

Transformation doesn't begin with pressure.
It begins with grounding.
Like a tree establishing its roots before bearing fruit,
Our lives flourish when they follow
The divine rhythms already written into creation.

Introduction - Part II: The Framework of Growth

A Journey Through the Tree of Life Within You

"I see people; they look like trees walking around." (Mark 8:24, NIV)

I. The Framework: Roots → Vine → Fruits → Seasons

True transformation isn't random, it follows a rhythm. The same sacred pattern found in creation is written into your story. You see it in trees, in the life of Christ, and in the very fabric of how we grow.

Introduction - Part II: The Framework of Growth

a. The Roots – The Seven Spirits of God
(See Isaiah 11:2)

Before anything grows upward, it must first grow deep. The Roots represent the Seven Spirits of God, seven dimensions of His Spirit (not separate spirits) that formed the character and ministry of Jesus:

- **The Spirit of the Lord**: God's active presence and power, transforming believers and empowering a life that reflects His glory (goodness).
- **The Spirit of Wisdom**: Divine intelligence and practical insight that helps life flow in alignment with God's truth.
- **The Spirit of Understanding**: A supernatural ability to grasp the meaning of truth, giving clarity for righteous living.
- **The Spirit of Counsel**: God's guidance and direction, enabling decisions that reflect His will and likeness.
- **The Spirit of Might**: Spiritual strength and boldness to fulfill God's will, even in the face of challenge.
- **The Spirit of Knowledge**: Revelatory insight into God's character and purposes, shaping holy living.
- **The Spirit of the Fear of the Lord**: A deep reverence that anchors us in awe and obedience, turning us away

from evil, not fear in a punitive sense, but a humble awareness of God's majesty.

These traits don't just describe God's Spirit, they shape who you're becoming. They steady you. They strengthen you. They anchor your life in something deeper than opinion or performance.

I came to know these roots not in a classroom, but in wilderness seasons. When I felt lost. Unseen. Uprooted. It was there, in the silence beneath the surface, that I realised: the Spirit doesn't just fill us, He forms us.

Introduction - Part II: The Framework of Growth

b. The Vine – Christ and the Seven Pillars

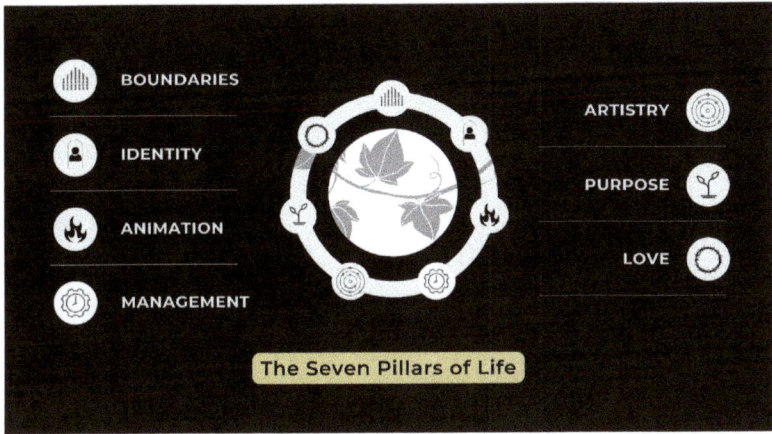

The Vine is Jesus Christ, the source of life *(John 15:5)*. He manifested the Roots as He walked on earth. To "*abide*" in Him means to remain connected in relationship and trust. Through Him, we grow by seven pillars. This is the journey you are about to walk:

- **Boundaries**: What we are bound to defines the shape of our lives.
- **Identity**: Our attachments shape who we become.
- **Animation**: From identity flows our self-expression, how we move, speak, and create.
- **Management**: Our animation influences how we order and steward what has been entrusted to us.
- **Artistry**: Through stewardship, life becomes a canvas painted from structure and principles.
- **Purpose**: Our artistry uncovers our calling, our God-given path that aligns our gifts with divine intention.
- **Love**: As we honour our boundaries, live in true identity, and walk in purpose, we are transformed to love at our highest capacity.

c. The Fruits – The Seven Areas of Life

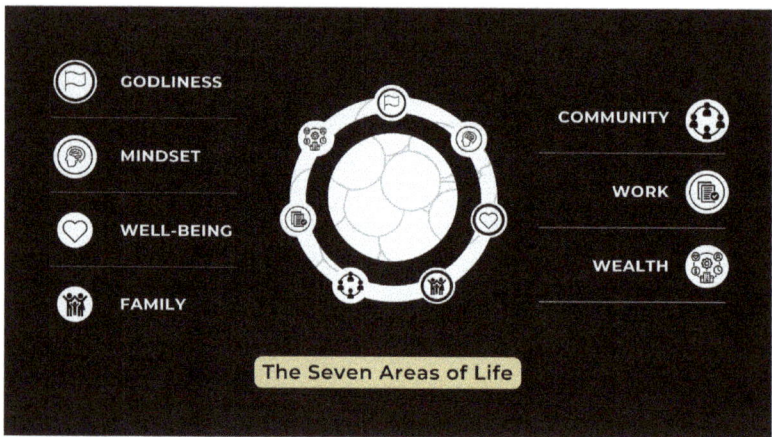

The Fruits are the visible expressions of a rooted, connected life. Not marks of perfection, but signs of alignment:
- **Godliness**: Anchoring your life in reverence *(Matthew 6:33)*.
- **Mindset**: Renewed thought patterns leading to clarity *(Romans 12:2)*.
- **Well-being**: Inner healing reflected in outer peace *(3 John 1:2)*.
- **Family**: Wholeness that transforms relationships *(Genesis 2:24)*.
- **Community**: Healing presence and fruitful fellowship *(Acts 2:42–47)*.
- **Work**: Purposeful excellence, not performance *(Colossians 3:23)*.
- **Wealth**: Stewarded provision, not pursued *(Proverbs 10:22)*.

These fruits grow from harmony, not hustle. When the Root is deep and the Vine is strong, fruit comes naturally, in season.

Introduction - Part II: The Framework of Growth

d. The Seasons – Embracing the Pattern of Growth

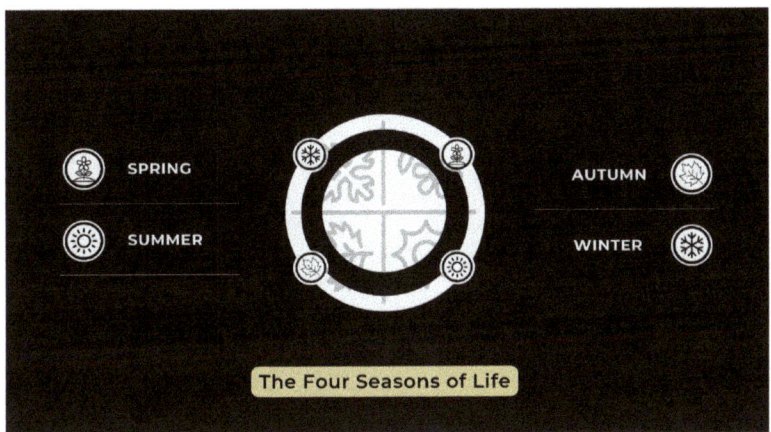

Growth is seasonal. Spring brings beginnings. Summer demands diligence. Autumn offers rewards. Winter invites pruning and rest.

As we move on, we later look above, to understand the seasons of life.

Growth isn't isolated. It doesn't happen on its own, without pressure, people, or timing.

Seasons shape everything from root to fruit.

II. A Bridge of Spirit-Filled Fruit

Between the Vine and the Fruits is something sacred, the Fruit of the Spirit *(Galatians 5:22–23)*. These are internal signs of spiritual life:

- **Love**: The foundation of growth *(1 Corinthians 13:4–7; 1 John 4:7–8)*
- **Joy**: Rooted gladness *(John 15:11; Romans 15:13)*
- **Peace**: Inner stillness *(Philippians 4:6–7; Isaiah 26:3)*
- **Patience**: Graceful endurance *(Colossians 3:12; James 1:4)*
- **Kindness**: Compassion in action *(Ephesians 4:32; Proverbs 11:17)*
- **Goodness**: Upright living *(Romans 12:21; Psalm 23:6)*
- **Faithfulness**: Steadfast loyalty *(Lamentations 3:22–23; Hebrews 11:1)*
- **Gentleness**: Strength restrained *(Matthew 11:29; Titus 3:2)*
- **Self-Control**: Spirit-led discipline *(2 Timothy 1:7; Proverbs 25:28)*

These virtues are not always fully formed in every believer. We are all growing from somewhere. The fruit isn't proof of perfection, it's evidence of surrender.

III. The Method: How This Book Will Aid Your Transformation

In the pages ahead, we'll journey through the seven pillars of the Vine: Boundaries; Identity; Animation; Management; Artistry; Purpose and Love. Each one is more than a concept, it's a living principle. A rhythm. A spiritual discipline that shapes how we live, lead, and love.

Introduction - Part II: The Framework of Growth

These pillars don't replace the Root, they reveal it. The Vine is how we practice abiding. It's how the invisible root of being anchored in God becomes visible in our everyday lives. These seven pillars are the outworking of a rooted life, showing up in how we handle pressure, relate to others, express ourselves, and build what lasts.

And they're not only personal, they're societal. When people grow in these areas, so do families. When leaders embody these truths, so do communities. When businesses align with these rhythms, culture shifts.

That's why this book isn't just a message, it's a method, here to help you frame life in a way you can be humble, rest, and flourish. Throughout this journey, I'll be drawing from a reimagined version of Bloom's Taxonomy, a framework designed not just for learning, but for lasting transformation.

Because it's not enough to know truth.
We must move from knowledge to comprehension, from application to analysis, From synthesis to evaluation,
And finally, into the sacred season of testing.

Testing is where truth becomes testimony.
Where what you've learned is refined in real life.
It's not failure, it's forming.

Through this rhythm, wisdom becomes embodied.
Principles become practice.
Revelation becomes resilience.

So whether you're an individual seeking clarity,
A leader shaping lives,
Or a visionary building something that outlives you,
This message is for you.
This is more than a book.

It's a vine of practice rooted in presence.
A structure for growth.
A blueprint for becoming.

IV. The Journey Begins

This book is part story, part reflection, part guide. It is not a pressure-filled message, but a planted one.

Because you were made to grow.
You were designed to be rooted, fruitful, whole.
You were always meant to become a tree of life in the middle of a weary world.

Let this be the turning of the soil.
Let this be the crack of the seed.
Let this be your sacred yes to a journey that won't just change your life,
But bring life to others through you.

A Prayer Before You Begin

God of all life and growth,
Prepare the soil of my heart.
Let every word in this book water what You've already planted in me.
Where I am weary, bring rest.
Where I am searching, bring clarity.
Where I am hardened, bring softness.

I open my heart to You now,
Ready not for perfection, but for presence.
Root me in love.
Anchor me in truth.
Make me fruitful in season.

Amen.

It's time to come alive.

Part I

Chapter 1: Boundaries - Guardrails of Growth

"In the beginning God created the heaven and the earth. And the earth was without form, and void; and darkness was upon the face of the deep. And the Spirit of God moved upon the face of the waters. And God said, Let there be light: and there was light. And God saw the light, that it was good: and God divided the light from the darkness. And God called the light Day, and the darkness he called Night. And the evening and the morning were the first day."
(Genesis 1:1–5, KJV)

What Are Boundaries?

Boundaries aren't walls to keep people out. They are fences that protect what's growing.

Boundaries aren't selfish. They are sacred. They are how love stays healthy, how peace stays planted.

Chapter 1: Boundaries - Guardrails of Growth

They define where you end and others begin. They draw a circle around what matters, so it can flourish in safety, not survive in stress.

We see this truth from the very first moments of creation. Before God filled the world, He formed it by establishing boundaries.

There are three foundational boundaries revealed in *Genesis 1:1* that shape how we live well:

Time: *"In the beginning..."*
God laid the foundation of time. Before rhythm, before sequence, before flow, He created the space for it all to unfold. Time was His first boundary, a beginning that made everything else possible.

- *For anything to exist, it must be sustained by something greater and operated by Someone greater. Time itself reveals the presence of the Everlasting. And if He is everlasting, then by nature, He must be infinite.*

Space: *"God created the heavens..."*
Space includes not just the physical, but the emotional, spiritual, and relational. Boundaries protect your atmosphere so that peace can settle and clarity can take root.

- *When you protect your space, you protect the conditions for growth.*

Matter: *"...and the earth."*
This refers to everything physical and tangible, your body and your resources. Boundaries help you manage what you carry, build, and give.

- *When you steward matter well, you multiply what God has given you.*

Only God exists beyond time, space, and matter. But within them, He invites us to cultivate life.

Boundaries aren't just helpful, they are holy. They don't box you in. They bless the space you've been given so you can grow like you were designed to.

But here's the truth: You won't honour boundaries until you understand what makes them sacred. What gives a boundary power isn't just logic or discipline, it's *reverence*.

Before you can guard your time, protect your space, or steward your body… You need to first recognise who it all belongs to.

That's where the **fear of the Lord** comes in, a holy reverence that aligns us with God's will and presence.

The Rooted Spirit Manifested: The Spirit of the Fear of the Lord

This is where it all begins.

The *Fear of the Lord* is the root. The boundary that anchors everything else. But it's not about being afraid.
It's about *reverence*.

It's the deep awareness that God is holy.
And if God is holy, then what He gives me is holy too:

- My time
- My body
- My choices
- My calling

The fear of the Lord doesn't make me shrink back,
It teaches me to stand taller.

It gives me dignity. It gives me discernment. It gives me boundaries.

Chapter 1: Boundaries - Guardrails of Growth

It says: *"You don't belong to everything. You've already said yes to Someone."*

That's why boundaries aren't just practical, they're prophetic. They quietly declare:

"I belong to God. And because I do, I live set apart."

It's not just a personal principle, it's a divine pattern. Before God created anything beautiful, He established where it belonged. He separated. He ordered. He spoke light into the chaos.

Let's look at how the very first boundary, Day One, set the tone for everything that followed.

Creation and the First Boundary

"In the beginning, God created the heavens and the earth..."
(Genesis 1:1 KJV)
But before He filled the earth with life,
He formed it, with boundaries.

The earth was formless, empty, and dark.
But the Spirit of God hovered over the chaos.
Then God spoke:
"Let there be light."
And just like that, order began.

That was the first day. And God called it good.

But notice:
Day One wasn't about progress.
It was about *perspective*.

God didn't build first.
He separated for clarity.

This Is Love, Not Religion

He drew lines:

- Light from darkness
- Time from timelessness
- Form from formlessness

The very first divine act was a *boundary*.

God showed us:
Before fruit can flourish,
Clarity must come.

Light, symbolising truth, order, and Christ Himself *(John 1:4–5)*, must be the reference point for everything that follows.

This is the power of boundaries.

They don't just organise life.
They invite *light* in.

They help us separate what is truly good from what is simply familiar.
They guide us toward what's aligned and away from what's distorted.

So if your life feels formless and void,
Maybe the answer isn't doing more.
Maybe it's making space.

Maybe it's time to let God separate what is divine... from what is merely distracting.

Because boundaries make room for God to say:
"Let there be light."

Over your time.
Over your relationships.
Over your priorities.
Over your identity.

Chapter 1: Boundaries - Guardrails of Growth

This isn't just a cosmic truth, it's a personal one.

We see it again in the life of Moses,
Before he ever led a nation.
Before he became a mouthpiece for God...
He had to learn to **withdraw**, to **wait**, and to let boundaries prepare him in the wilderness.

A Living Example: Moses Withdraws *(Exodus 2)*

Before Moses was a deliverer,
He was a man in conflict.
Torn between cultures.
Misaligned in identity.
Without emotional or spiritual boundaries.

In *Exodus 2*, Moses sees an Egyptian beating a Hebrew.
He acts, not from purpose, but from impulse.
He kills the Egyptian and hides the body in the sand.

It looked like courage.
But it was confusion.
It was justice without wisdom.
Passion without restraint.

Moses hadn't yet learned to channel identity through calling, only through pain.

So he ran.
Not just from failure, but from exposure.

But what looked like exile was actually a setup.
God was pulling him out, not to punish, but to prepare.

This Is Love, Not Religion

In Midian, Moses didn't lead, he listened.
He didn't perform, he learned to be present.
He wasn't visible, he was made invisible on purpose.

There, tending sheep, walking hills, living in rhythm,
Moses began to change.

He was learning what the palace never taught him:

Boundaries birth wisdom.
Boundaries build strength.
Boundaries prepare you for weight.

Because what God was calling him to carry
Couldn't be sustained by passion alone.
It needed patience.
It needed formation.
It needed roots.

Moses isn't the only one.

Many of us carry callings we feel,
But we haven't yet formed the boundaries that can hold them.

We long to help.
To heal.
To be used by God.

But without clear lines, even our best intentions leak.

Let's explore what happens when life is lived without boundaries,
When love is offered without shape.

The Scenario: A Life Without Lines

You wake up already overwhelmed.
Your phone is buzzing.

Chapter 1: Boundaries - Guardrails of Growth

Emails. Notifications. Expectations.
And the day hasn't even begun.

You want to say no, but guilt creeps in.
Are you being selfish?
Are you just weak?

So you say yes. Again.

And by the end of the day, you're not empty from apathy,
You're empty from overgiving.

Not because you didn't care,
But because you didn't protect what matters.

This is the cycle many of us know too well.
Stretched.
Scattered.
Disconnected from ourselves.

We want to be loving.
Helpful.
Successful.

But without boundaries...

Love gets diluted.
Purpose gets distracted.
Identity gets distorted.

When you don't know where you end,
You'll give pieces of yourself away without realising it.

You'll give time where you have none.
Energy where you've already poured out.
Access to people who were never meant to hold sacred space.

Boundaries don't make you selfish.
They keep you from becoming someone you were never meant to be.

This Is Love, Not Religion

If you've lived this, if your yes has cost you peace,
You're not alone.

I've been there.

I didn't learn boundaries from a book.
I learned them the hard way,
Through pressure, collapse, and eventually... freedom.

Let me show you what God taught me when my life fell apart,
And how He used brokenness to build something sacred.

My Turning Point: The Birthing Of Freedom

1. The Early Observation: The Weight of the World

Even as a child, I noticed something: People always looked tired. Heavy. Weighed down by life, money, family, and expectations.

I remember thinking, *"Surely life isn't meant to be this exhausting."*

But I was a child... Naive. And one day, I would carry that same weight for myself.

Life hit hard.

My journey shifted unexpectedly when I was offered a basketball scholarship in L.A.
It happened in a Nike store in Las Vegas. A coach saw two tall guys during the AAU season, and suddenly, an opportunity opened.

But here's the truth: I wasn't that good. I was raw. Unpolished. Carried more by favour than by skill.

Chapter 1: Boundaries - Guardrails of Growth

I accepted the offer. And still... something felt exciting, distant and missing.

I was growing, but unbalanced,
Talent with no tenderness.
Focus without compassion.
A platform, but no honour.

The boundaries I did have were built by a boy on a mission,
Eyes fixed on selfish ambition.

I longed for love, but gave and received it in broken ways.
I used and felt used.

I clung to distractions I could control,
Preferring noise over stillness,
Because silence asked questions I wasn't ready to answer.

I wasn't leading my life,
I was in the passenger seat.
Intentional only in my narrow wants,
Aimless with the people around me,
Blind to the bigger picture God was trying to show me.

---

2. The Collapse: When It All Fell Apart

Years later, I graduated in Texas. Everything looked promising.

A girl I loved.
A business idea gaining traction.
A job offer in retail leadership.

But here's the truth behind that love,
It was fractured and fragile.
We filled each other's insecurities,
And our imagination wandered into spaces never meant for us.

How did it happen?

---

3. How Did It Happen?

Let me take you on an undercurrent journey within this journey.
She flew out to see me.
Finally, time alone together.
Heartbeats quickened.
Excitement crept in.
Nerves shrieked under the surface.

And then it came,
A voice. Clear. Steady. Holy.
"No."

I knew it was from above,
But I was already embracing what was below,
Already holding close the one who felt near.

What I didn't see in that moment
Was that He was protecting us from each other.
We were fiery for one another in ways that felt intoxicating,
Passion. Lust. Longing. Desire, all fulfilled.

But what burns quickly dies quicker.
We trespassed God's no,
And the time to pay the price came.

Later, I remained in Texas.
She returned to London.
Passion turned to frustration.
Lust to dissatisfaction.
Longing to disappointment.
Desire left us thirsty.

Arrogance whispered she would always be there.
But years passed,

Chapter 1: Boundaries - Guardrails of Growth

And I lived in the consequence of disobedience to the Lord's boundaries.
Heartbroken.
Yet still called.
And by His mercy and grace,
I was led to grow instead of die in the wilderness.

In those years, He redefined love for me.
Strangely, I loved her more when we weren't together.
Not selfishly, but selflessly.
I wanted more for her, not from her.
We came close to rekindling the flame once,
But it was never meant to be.

The healing was painfully slow,
Exactly the pace required to teach a lifetime's lesson.

Have I learned and moved forward? Yes.
Would I change anything? No.
Although ignorance showed the need for knowledge.
And that helped me respect His boundaries.

Now I am a living testimony,
Able to help others make better decisions.
The pain was necessary
To make me necessary for my purpose.

I have made several mistakes,
But I can never go back to who I was.

I am indebted to God for His timing and provision,
For teaching me to love Him more
From a position and posture I would never have chosen.

---

4. The Return to the Season

But stubborn hearts need hard lessons.

That was the journey within the journey.
Now, back in that season...

So, just like that, it all vanished.

The girl left.
The business faded.
The job? Delayed for months.

---

5. Stripped and Empty

I was broke. Heartbroken. Down. Sleeping on the floor in an apartment I couldn't afford, no furniture, no food, no money.

It all mirrored how my life felt: Stripped and empty. Just quiet. And questions.

My mother (unaware) sent me £100 a month. Enough to survive, barely.

I learnt quickly:
The struggle builds character.
That season brought clarity.

---

6. The Crossroads: One Decision

One night, lying on the floor listening to R&B,
I realised I had two choices.

One path:
Go dark.
Do whatever it takes to survive, lie, steal, compromise.

The other path felt...
Like a king.

Chapter 1: Boundaries - Guardrails of Growth

Cleaner.
Right.
True.

A beginning of someone new in me,
Who was still me.

Humbled. Empty. Defeated.
I made a decision: Jesus.

I said in my heart:
"What do I have to lose?"

And then… I heard His voice within.
"Be patient."

It wasn't my voice.
It was Presence.
Familiar, holy, undeniable.

I contended:
"I'm the most patient person I know."

But the voice returned, firmer:
"No. Be patient."

I turned my head. There it was, a poster on the wall:
Perseverance.

And I knew…
What was ahead would take endurance. Not hustle.
Not shortcuts.
But patience and surrender.

Christ began to teach me about His boundaries: The fear of the Lord.
Virtues.
Values.
High standards, not by effort, but by alignment.

7. The Promise: I Will Give You Your Life

It happened quietly.
Not a thought.
Not a dream.
A promise.

"I will give you your life."

I didn't fully understand it,
But I believed it.

It wasn't just about having a life,
It was about receiving the one I was always meant to live.

A life of alignment.
Of honour.
Of rest and rooted identity.

Not just surviving, but becoming.

8. Awakening: A New Way of Seeing

That promise began to clear my vision. I started valuing people, not for what they could do for me, but for who they were.

I wanted more than to be "a good man." I wanted to be a king, But not the world's version of royalty.

In time, I realised what I really wanted: To be like Jesus.

A King who leads through humility. Who walks with purpose. Who lives with love and boundaries at the same time.

9. Revelation: Boundaries Birth Freedom

Eventually, I saw it: I wasn't growing, I was grinding.
Striving instead of surrendering.

I had to learn:
Even sacred things become burdens when boundaries are missing.

It wasn't a vacation that healed me.
It was a revelation:

Love has shape.
Freedom has form.
Even God operates within the boundary of His Word.

That truth flipped my entire life.

10. The Prodigal Return: Restoration Through Boundaries

I saw how I had opened doors I shouldn't have.
I gave access to sacred spaces, my time, my emotions, even my body, without discernment.

I crossed lines.
And felt the weight of shame.

But like the prodigal son, I returned.
Not perfect.
But honest.

And God met me not with punishment, but with restoration.

Even in my mess, I saw His mercy.
Even in my failure, I felt His favour.

---

11. Discernment: Seeing the Intangible

In my return, God taught me to see what can't be seen.

Lust wasn't just attraction.
It was the collision of unmet needs, emotions, wounds and desires,
All crossing invisible lines.

Without virtue, values break down.
And without values, boundaries collapse.

I needed more than behaviour change.
I needed heart clarity.

---

12. Vision: Boundaries That Reflect God's Design

And that's when I saw it:

Boundaries aren't barriers to joy.
They are the **backbone** of freedom.

They don't shut life out,
They hold life together.

They uphold families.
They safeguard communities.

They are the framework for nations
They reflect the Kingdom.

Chapter 1: Boundaries - Guardrails of Growth

Through His Spirit, I realised:
Clarity is possible.
Peace is possible.
Prosperity is possible.

But only through order.

Before I learned about boundaries,
God established them in me.
That victory is His.

Now?
He's positioned me to help others build what I had to learn the hard way:

That boundaries, rightly built,
Aren't restrictions,
They're reflections.

You were made in His image.
You were made for shape, for honour, for freedom.

Let's bring it into daily life.

Because boundaries don't just live in theology or testimony,
They show up in your calendar, your relationships, your yes and your no.

Let's make it practical.

Practicing Boundaries in Real Life

Two books that were later brought to my attention about boundaries were:
***Boundaries* by Dr. Henry Cloud** and ***The Awe of God* by John Bevere**.

This Is Love, Not Religion

They aligned with what the Spirit had already been revealing to me:
That boundaries aren't legalistic, they're **liberating**.
And that the **fear of the Lord** isn't about being afraid,
It's about reverence.

Reverence shifts how you carry what's been entrusted to you.
It makes your time holy.
Your energy, sacred.
Your choices, weighty, not burdensome, but meaningful.

It changes the question from:

"Can I do this?"
to
"Would God be pleased with how I'm handling this?"

That question becomes a boundary all on its own.

As I've grown, I've come to see that healthy boundaries are shaped by four core values.
Each one makes love clearer, not colder.

Love

Message:
Love is not proven by what you burn to keep others warm.
True love gives fully, but not foolishly.

Parable:
There was a man who kept a small lantern at his door.
Each night, travellers would come seeking its light.
He welcomed them, always.
He gave what he had, warmth, stories, and comfort.

But as more people came,
He grew afraid of disappointing them.
So he fed the flame with pieces of his own furniture.

Chapter 1: Boundaries - Guardrails of Growth

A leg from the table.
A scrap from the shelf.
Part of the roof.

The light never went out,
But neither did the damage.
Until one stormy night,
The house collapsed around the lantern,
And no one could stay, not even him.

Instruction:
Do the best you can do with who you are and what you have for your fellow neighbour and yourself.

How it helps with boundaries:
Love sets the standard for what you give and what you preserve. When you act from love, you don't overextend to please, you give from overflow, not obligation.
It helps you stay grounded in your capacity, own your needs and resist the pressure to perform or be perfect for others. It draws a line between responsibility and over-responsibility.

Reflect:
Are you preserving the house that hosts your light, or slowly feeding it to the fire?

Honesty

Message:
Honesty doesn't expose you to shame,
It frees you from performing.

Parable:
A woman was given a mirror unlike any other.
It didn't just reflect the surface,
It showed her heart, her fatigue, her truth.
But over time, she grew tired of what she saw.

This Is Love, Not Religion

So she dimmed the lights.
She spoke cheerfully.
She kept busy.

Visitors came and said, "You look well."
And she nodded.
Because it was easier to agree than explain.

But the cracks didn't fade,
They widened beneath the silence.

One day, she faced the mirror again.
Not to correct the image.
Not to smile through it.
But to see what was real.

And in that quiet honesty,
She exhaled,
For the first time in a long time.

It wasn't the mask that gave her strength,
It was the courage to take it off.

Instruction:
Be honest with yourself, your neighbour and in what you do.

How it helps with boundaries:
Honesty reveals your true limits and needs. It keeps you from pretending and invites others to meet you in truth.
It creates space to say, "I can't," without shame and helps you live in alignment instead of performance. It draws the line between what's authentic and what's tolerated out of pressure.

Reflect:
Where have you been hiding pain behind politeness?

Chapter 1: Boundaries - Guardrails of Growth

Respect

Message:
Respect is not how wide you open the door,
It's how clearly you define the threshold.

Parable:
A man owned a quiet house on a busy street.
He kept his door open, always.
Neighbours came freely.
Some stayed too long.
Some brought muddy shoes.
Others moved furniture, rearranged his space.
He said nothing.
He told himself, *"It's just kindness."*
Until one day, he walked into his own living room
And didn't recognise it anymore.

So he closed the door.
Not in bitterness,
But in wisdom.

Now, when people knock, he still welcomes them.
But he invites them in with intention,
Clear steps.
Gentle boundaries.
Mutual honour.

And something changed:
The conversations became lighter.
The space stayed sacred.
And the relationships grew stronger.

Instruction:
Respect what you stand for: others, yourself and what you have.

How it helps with boundaries:
Respect creates healthy distance and honour. It lets you value yourself enough to say no and value others enough not to

manipulate or control.
It allows you to stand in authentically with grace and recognises that you don't have to compromise your standards to be kind.

Reflect:
Where have you confused being agreeable with being aligned?

Fun

Message:
Fun isn't lost in boundaries.
It's protected by them.

Parable:
A group of friends gathered every weekend to play a game.
No one set rules.
"No need," they said. *"We trust each other."*

At first, it was laughter.
But soon, someone bent the truth to win.
Another grew loud when they lost.
One walked off. Another stayed silent.
And what began in joy,
Ended in tension.

The next week, they tried again.
But this time,
They made space for clarity.
Clear turns. Fair play. Boundaries for the sake of everyone.

And the laughter returned.
Not because there were no limits.
But because now, everyone felt safe within them.

Chapter 1: Boundaries - Guardrails of Growth

Instruction:
Have fun being challenged, making mistakes and being creative in your ways.

How it helps with boundaries:
Fun without boundaries leads to chaos, but fun within boundaries creates safe freedom. It protects the joy and keeps it life-giving, not reckless.
Boundaries make space for play that doesn't harm others or yourself, helping you stay grounded in self-respect while enjoying spontaneity.

Reflect:
Where have you let fear of control rob you of structure that brings joy?

From Fun to Love

Boundaries don't begin with restriction,
They begin with freedom.

It's like when you enter an environment, home, streets, business, church.
You can feel how much love is present
By the healthy fun that's allowed.
But that fun only feels safe
Because it's underlaid by respect, rooted in honesty, and centred in love.

Think of it like a cylindrical pyramid:
Fun is the invitation.
Respect is the structure.
Honesty is the foundation.
Love is the centre.

The deeper the boundary,
The freer the joy.

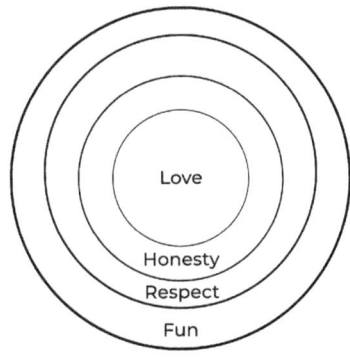

Boundaries don't box you in.
They **bless** what's within.
They help you love like God does,
Fully, truthfully and without losing yourself in the process.

So what's the real win here?

Closing Thoughts

In this chapter, we uncovered the **sacred nature of boundaries**, not as restrictions, but as divine distinctions. Just as God separated light from darkness on **Day One**, He brings clarity and peace into our lives through healthy, Spirit-led boundaries.

We explored how boundaries govern **three key domains**: **Time; Space and Matter.**
God created these domains to house His will and we are called to honour them through intentional rhythms, protective environments and Spirit-filled stewardship.

We learned that boundaries are the first step toward fruitfulness.
God doesn't pour into what hasn't first been formed.
Form precedes filling.
Structure precedes overflow.

We looked at the **Spirit of the Fear of the Lord**, who gives us reverence, wisdom, and spiritual clarity to say yes to what aligns with God and no to what doesn't.

But we also saw this:
Where God sets boundaries to bring life, the enemy works subtly to erode them.
Through false freedoms, cultural compromise, and spiritual numbness, he leads many to mistake bondage for liberty.

Chapter 1: Boundaries - Guardrails of Growth

A life without boundaries isn't just disordered, it's vulnerable to deception.

That's why drawing the line matters.
Boundaries are not legalism, they are light.

Through creation, Moses' story and our own lives, we see that boundaries are not a limitation,
They are a platform for **God's movement** to flow freely.

Next we saw, I didn't learn boundaries through discipline alone.
I learned them when everything fell apart,
and God rebuilt me with lines that brought peace, not pressure.

Boundaries are sacred.
They are not a wall to hide behind.
They are a gate to grow within.

They create space for the Spirit to dwell,
And for truth to take root.

To draw a line is not to be distant,
It's to be defined.

When we protect our space,
We protect our peace.
And when we honour our time,
We honour the One who gave it.

This is where freedom begins,
Not in doing everything,
But in **guarding what matters most**.

Because once we know where we end and where God begins,
We're ready to discover who we truly are.

Next, we step into **Identity**,
Where our boundaries make room for our becoming,
And our name echoes the One who made us.

Prayer Decreeing Boundaries: Standing in Sacred Space

I am not called to chaos, I am called to live in order and peace *(1 Corinthians 14:33)*.

I am a steward of my time, my space and my energy.
I honour the boundaries God has set around my life,
Because they protect what is sacred.

I was created with purpose *(Ephesians 2:10)*,
Set apart to walk in wisdom and truth *(Proverbs 4:7)*.
I no longer say yes to everything, I say yes to what aligns with heaven.

I am not governed by pressure, guilt, or fear.
I am led by the Spirit of God *(Romans 8:14)*,
Who gives me clarity, conviction and confidence.

I protect my peace.
I guard my atmosphere.
I honour the space God has given me to grow.

I do not apologise for walking in truth.
I do not shrink back to be more acceptable.
I am set apart, not stretched thin.

I live with purpose.
I choose what is excellent *(Philippians 1:10)*.
I stand in sacred space, because I belong to a holy God.

In Jesus' name.
Amen.

Chapter 1: Boundaries - Guardrails of Growth

Chapter 2: Identity - Becoming Who We Really Are

"And God said, Let there be a firmament in the midst of the waters, and let it divide the waters from the waters. And God made the firmament, and divided the waters which were under the firmament from the waters which were above the firmament: and it was so. And God called the firmament Heaven. And the evening and the morning were the second day."
(Genesis 1:6–8, KJV)

What Is Identity?

Identity isn't something you earn.
It's something you uncover.

It's not an achievement.
It's a revelation.

Chapter 2: Identity - Becoming Who We Really Are

At your core, you are not random.
You are an image-bearer.
Formed to reflect God.
Not just to exist, but to echo His presence on the earth.

Whether you believe or you're still exploring, know this:
Your identity isn't a coincidence.
It's a calling.

From a biblical lens, identity begins when we attach to Christ,
the Way, the Truth, and the Life (John 14:6).

From a practical lens, identity grows when we stop outsourcing our worth
To applause, status, or appearance,
And instead begin living from unshakable virtues.

That's what I began to explore:

- What virtues did Christ embody?
- What did God reveal about Himself?
- What did He want me to reflect?

These weren't religious rules.
They were truths, replicable, radiant, and ready for anyone who wants them.

Because when identity is unclear:
We chase significance in performance.
We reach for validation in applause.
We mask insecurity with image.

But when we know who we are,
We stop performing.
And we start living.

Identity becomes a foundation:
For consistency.
For clarity.
For confidence.

This Is Love, Not Religion

But identity doesn't grow in isolation.
It grows within the boundaries we keep.

When we create boundaries that guard godly virtues,
Like love, patience, and self-control.
We're not just protecting ourselves.
We're partnering with God.

Because here's the mystery:
We cultivate the space...
But *He* creates the environment.

God uses seasons to stretch us,
To shape us,
To grow the character that reflects His name.

Our role isn't to force fruit.
It's to tend the soil.

To honour the space we've been given,
So that what He wants to grow can take root.

That's where identity truly begins:
In the sacred space where God meets our yes.

If identity is where your *being* begins,
Then the Spirit of Knowledge brings light to that.

Let's explore how God reveals who we are,
Not through noise, but through knowing.

Chapter 2: Identity - Becoming Who We Really Are

The Rooted Spirit Manifested: The Spirit of Knowledge

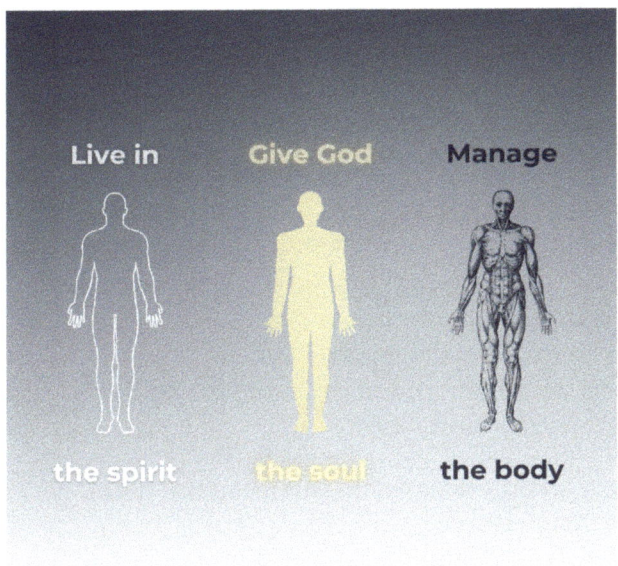

God breathed His Spirit into Adam's body. Identity.

The body, lifeless on its own, needed a firmament where identity could grow and purpose could take root. Soul.

The dust of the ground was made alive, becoming a reflection of the breath within, a temple for God to dwell in communion. Body.

The *Spirit of Knowledge* doesn't just give you facts.
It gives you *truth*.

It brings light to who God is,
And in doing so, it holds up a mirror to who you are.

This Is Love, Not Religion

This Spirit doesn't speak with noise.
It speaks with clarity.
It awakens divine insight,
Helping you see what is eternal,
What is holy,
And what has always been within you.

It reveals the value God placed in you,
A value no title, trauma, or trend can define.

It strips away the false labels.
It breaks inherited lies.
And it whispers deep into your spirit:

*"You are known. You are chosen.
You are formed in My image.
And I call you by name."*

That's why identity is not something you construct.
It's something *revealed*.

It doesn't begin with performance.
It begins with *presence*.

Because the world gives you reality,
But God gives you truth.

Reality is shaped by culture,
By family history,
By trends, trauma, and timing.

It hands you labels.
It forms your survival strategies.
And many of us adapt just to get by.

But truth?
Truth is what *God says* about you.

And that truth is not just heard.
It is *revealed by* the Spirit of Knowledge.

Chapter 2: Identity - Becoming Who We Really Are

You can live from the knowledge of good and evil,
Always measuring, comparing, striving...

Or you can live from the *knowledge of God*,
Rooted in His voice,
Shaped by His Spirit,
Transformed by His gaze.

One turns you into a reflection of the world around you.
The other turns you into who you were always meant to be:

A child of God.

This isn't just theological, it's tangible.
We see it in the very act of creation.

Because before identity was ever expressed,
It was protected. It was formed in space,
Stretched in separation,
And revealed through distinction.

Let's look at what God did on Day Two,
And how identity was hidden in the heavens.

Living from the Garden: Knowing vs Being

When Jesus rose from the dead, Mary mistook Him for a gardener.
That wasn't random, it was revelation.

Humanity began in a garden.
And Christ, the second Adam, was revealing the restoration of what was lost.
He wasn't just alive again, He was cultivating something new.
A new covenant.
A new creation.
A new way of knowing.

This Is Love, Not Religion

But notice this: in the original garden, there were two distinct trees,
One of Life,
And one of the Knowledge of Good and Evil (Genesis 2:9).

The tree of knowledge wasn't evil in itself.
But reaching for it apart from God was.
That's what happens when we chase head knowledge
Instead of the Spirit of Knowledge.

Many of us do this without realising.
We think knowing more makes us better.
We cling to facts, degrees, doctrines,
But sometimes we forget to become the truth we claim to understand.

Ask yourself:
Have you ever felt like you knew better,
But weren't being better?

That's the difference between information and revelation.

The Spirit of Knowledge doesn't just tell you what's right,
It leads you into how to live.
Humbly.
Wisely.
Fruitfully.

It takes what is hidden and makes it known,
Not to puff us up, but to plant us deep.

That's why Scripture says,
"Knowledge puffs up, but love builds up" (1 Corinthians 8:1).
Because the goal of godly knowledge isn't status.
It's transformation.

In Genesis 2:15, before sin ever entered the world,
God gave Adam a call:
"Tend and keep the garden."

Chapter 2: Identity - Becoming Who We Really Are

That wasn't about control.
It was about care.

Adam named the animals.
Not from intellect alone,
but from relationship.
Intimacy produced insight.
And insight revealed identity, his and theirs.

Knowledge with God was never about accumulation.
It was about alignment.

And it still is.

To live by the Spirit of Knowledge today is to tend your life
Like a garden.
To guard what's been planted.
To keep the weeds of pride and comparison from choking what's growing.

This is what it looks like to live from true knowledge:

- **Be fruitful**: Let your life produce virtue, not just opinions.
- **Multiply:** Share truth, not just content.
- **Replenish:** Be a restorer, not just a consumer.
- **Subdue:** Take authority over chaos, starting with your thoughts.
- **Have dominion:** Lead with love, not ego.

This isn't theory.
It's design.

You weren't made to carry data.
You were made to carry presence.

To reflect not just what you know,
But Who you walk with.

So don't settle for eating the fruit of knowledge
If it disconnects you from the Tree of Life.

Come back to the Gardener.
Let Him teach you how to tend what's inside.
Let Him show you that wisdom is more than knowing,
It's becoming.

Because when the Spirit of Knowledge is alive in you,
Your life becomes a garden again,
A place of order, beauty, and divine presence.

Creation and the Formation of Identity

"And God said, 'Let there be a vault between the waters to separate water from water.' And God called the vault 'sky.'"
(Genesis 1:6–8, NIV)

On Day Two, God didn't fill.
He separated.

What was once blended in chaos,
He divided with intention,
Creating space.
Creating identity.

The firmament (the vault) was a holy distinction.
A boundary between the waters above and below.
A line drawn by heaven,
Not to control, but to clarify.
To restore in the way of the will of God.

This is the process of identity:

- **Separation.**
- **Identification.**
- **Restoration.**

Chapter 2: Identity - Becoming Who We Really Are

RESTORATION

IDENTIFICATION

SEPARATION

This Is Love, Not Religion

God often separates us before He reveals us.
Not to isolate, but to prepare.

He pulls us out,
From the noise,
From the familiar,
From roles that no longer fit.

It can feel like loss.
But it's really *alignment*.

Because when you release what's false,
You make room for what's true.

When you surrender what's worn out,
You give space for what's eternal to rise.
Not by striving,
But by surrender.

And here's the question:

Would you rather live uncomfortably in truth,
Or comfortably in a lie?

I chose truth.
And yes, it cost me comfort,
But it birthed freedom.

The Hebrew word for *firmament* means *"to stretch, to hammer out."*
That's what the growth of identity often feels like,
Uncomfortable, uncertain, yet true.

A picture of faith in motion.

It forms in the tension.
In the stretching.
In the wilderness seasons of *"not yet."*

Chapter 2: Identity - Becoming Who We Really Are

It's not shallow.
It's not status.
It's not your title or your role.

Your identity is like the sacred space between heaven and earth
That God breathes into.

Formed by Him.
Held by Him.
Named by Him.

Even in the unseen,
Even when it feels like nothing's happening,
God is forming who you really are.

If you've ever wrestled with identity in the middle of transition,
You're not alone.

Moses did too.
Long before he delivered others,
He had to let God deliver him,
From false names,
From buried shame,
And from a story that wasn't his to carry.

Let's go there next.

A Living Example: Moses Wrestles with Who He Is *(Exodus 3–4)*

God didn't speak to Moses by title.
Not by mistake.
Not by résumé.
Not by shame.

This Is Love, Not Religion

He called him by name:
"Moses, Moses."

And Moses answered,
"Here I am."

Then God said,

"Take off your sandals, for the place where you stand is holy ground."
(Exodus 3:5)

This was more than a moment.
It was a mirror.

For forty years, Moses buried his identity beneath fear and failure.
He ran from his past.
He questioned his worth.
He settled into obscurity.

But in this moment, God didn't just speak *to* Moses,
He spoke *into* him.

God wasn't looking for a perfect man.
He was calling forth a *positioned* one.

Still, Moses hesitated:

"Who am I that I should go?"
"What if they don't believe me?"
"I am slow of speech..."

He measured his future by his past.
He tried to qualify the call by disqualifying himself.

But God didn't give him a pep talk.
He gave him *presence*.

Chapter 2: Identity - Becoming Who We Really Are

"I will be with you."
(Exodus 3:12)

That's the turning point.

Because when reality says, *"You're not enough,"*
Truth says, *"I AM."*

When the world sees a fugitive,
God sees a deliverer.

When others see what you've lost,
God sees what He planted in you,
Before you ever ran.

At the burning bush, Moses took off his sandals.
And with them, he laid down the labels.
The shame.
The excuses.

This is where identity is uncovered,
Not in perfection,
But in *proximity*.

Close to the One who knew your name,
Before the world tried to rename you.

But what happens when that clarity isn't there?

What happens when you wake up unsure of who you are,
Tossed between roles,
Stretched between expectations,
And silently wondering,
"Where do I fit?"

Let's talk about the ache of the unsettled soul.

The Scenario: The Unsettled Soul

You wake up unsure.
Not just about what to do,
But about who you are.

You scroll.
You compare.
You see snapshots of curated lives and wonder,
"Am I enough?"
"Am I doing it right?"
"Am I becoming who I'm meant to be?"

You move between roles,
Leader. Partner. Parent. Friend,
But still feel the subtle ache underneath:

You're not fully you.

That's the ache of identity unrest.

It's the quiet tension of being shaped by everything around you,
But anchored by nothing within you.

Without a clear core,
You perform to feel peace.
You chase affirmation instead of alignment.
You wear roles instead of resting in truth.

And the more you shift to meet expectations,
The more disconnected you feel.

This is what happens when identity is outsourced,
When you build your sense of self on applause, image, or need.

You become reactive instead of rooted.
Exhausted instead of established.
Present, but not whole.

Chapter 2: Identity - Becoming Who We Really Are

And even if no one sees it,
You know the feeling.

Because peace doesn't come from being praised.
It comes from being planted.

I know this tension well.
I've lived it.

And it wasn't a podcast, a post, or a moment of success that changed me.

It was surrender.

Let me show you what happened when I finally stopped performing...
And started getting honest.

My Turning Point: The Surrendering Of Self

1. A Different Kind of Inheritance

I was speaking to a friend once,
And they mentioned how in times of trouble,
They'd remember who their dad was,
A strength, an affirmation,
A mirror of who they were meant to be.

I never knew people did that.
But here I was, doing it all along.
I didn't grow up with a knowing of who I really was,
I pieced together my identity through what I saw.
I looked to coaches, TV, friends, and athletes,
People who seemed confident, clear, respected.
They showed me who I could be,
Or so I thought.

2. The Ego I Built

It gave me a foundation,
But it was weak.
A stitched-together ego.
Not formed in truth,
But framed by fear,
Shaped by survival.

Because I didn't like who I was,
I became afraid of facing it.
Stillness brought shame.
So I buried shame with pride.
Pride told me I was fine.
Good enough.
Doing ok.

To protect that pride, I built an ego,
Not from truth,
But from what was loudest.
The streets.
The screens.
The voices of people
Who looked confident but carried chaos.
Over time, the ego wasn't armour.
It became identity.
And in becoming it,
I made myself my own god.

3. The Culture that Shaped Me

I numbed what hurt.
I silenced what was soft.
And I fed my fear and pride
With what the culture handed me:

Chapter 2: Identity - Becoming Who We Really Are

Music, shows, sport, distraction.

The world became my grower.
Society, my dealer.
And I was the user.
But I was starving.

I drifted through life aimlessly.
With no boundaries.
No clarity.
No anchor.

Until the trials came.
And the ego couldn't carry me anymore.

---

4. The Voice of the Father

It was then that something deeper called me.
Not just God, not just King,
But Father.

The shift came when I stopped believing every thought
And started listening to my feelings differently.
I didn't disown them.
I discerned them.
Because feelings aren't facts,
They're signals.
And if left unchecked,
They'll drive you to build a life based on survival
Instead of truth.

---

5. Virtue Over Emotion

I started to realise:
Doing the right thing doesn't always feel good.

And feeling good doesn't always mean you're right.
God does what's right,
Even when it doesn't feel good.
And if His love is consistent,
Then mine can be too.

Love is a standard, not a mood.
And when I let virtue lead,
Instead of fear, pride, or the need for approval,
Healing began.

---

6. The Sacred Surrender

But there was more.
A deeper prompting.
A moment in silence,
When God said:
"Write your life."
Not the version I curated.
The real one.

So I did.
I wrote what I saw.
What I wanted.
What I hoped for in others and in me.
I wrote down the random.
The embarrassing.
Even the things I was scared to want or achieve.
And when it was all there, raw, honest, and uncovered,
I gave it to Him.

---

7. The Exchange of Scripts

I surrendered not just my identity,
But the script I had written for my life.

That act, simple, silent, and unseen,
Changed everything.
Because in surrendering the story,
I discovered the real Author.

I stopped trying to invent myself,
And started learning how to receive myself.

---

8. The Daily Death

Dying to self is not a dramatic moment,
It's a daily decision.

It's choosing to forgive when pride wants to win.
It's saying sorry, even when your ego aches.
It's resisting the comfort of carnal patterns,
And choosing heaven's rhythm instead.

To die to self
Is to lay down the false ways of being,
So that holiness can rise.

It is not passive,
It's deeply intentional.

A sacred resolve that says:
"I will live set apart.
I will be holy unto the Lord."

---

9. The Foundation Season

And He didn't rebuild me in a day.
He took me through a process.
Like a good Father does.
I remember the word in my spirit during that season:

"Foundation."

He was building mine.

---

10. Men of Excellence

In my early years of separation,
I found myself on fire to learn.
I consumed hours of reading what awakened me,
Steve Jobs, Ray Dalio, Napoleon Hill, Charles G. Koch.
Voices of excellence.
I related to their mindset.
To their standards.

Then I came across Tony Robbins,
Bold, driven, focused on becoming more.
He lit something in me.
A call to raise my standards.
To change how I moved in the world.

---

11. The Thread to Christ

Tony led me to Jim Rohn.
Witty. Grounded.
And without forcing anything,
He mentioned Jesus.
Not as a doctrine.
But as someone worth admiring.

It was enough.

Jesus made sense to me.
Not as a religion.
But as a rhythm.
A way.

Chapter 2: Identity - Becoming Who We Really Are

Later, I'd learn Jim Rohn's mentor was Earl Shoaff.
Another Christian.
Another thread in the tapestry God was weaving.

God used all of it.
Not to replace the Gospel,
But to prepare me for it.

---

12. The Father Who Found Me

I didn't grow up with a biological father,
But through these men,
God began showing me who I was,
And whose I was.

I learned that even outside the church walls,
He was still speaking.
Still drawing.
Still building.

---

13. The True Knowing

And when I finally met Him,
Not just as Lord,
But as Father,
I became unshakable.

Not because of what I knew,
But because I finally knew who knew me.

He was never trying to make me religious.
He was trying to make me whole.

And from that wholeness,
He planted the true identity I'd always been searching for.

Practicing Identity in Real Life

Before you do anything to shape your identity,
Pray for wisdom.

Ask the Holy Spirit to guide your thoughts,
Expose false beliefs,
And lead you into truth.

Because identity isn't just built through effort,
It's revealed by grace.

And it was by His Spirit that I learned how to cultivate mine.

Here's how you can begin:

1. Create an Environment of Truth

*"Finally, brothers and sisters, whatever is true, whatever is noble,
whatever is right, whatever is pure, whatever is lovely, whatever is admirable—
if anything is excellent or praiseworthy— think about such things."*
(Philippians 4:8, NIV)

"My people are destroyed for lack of knowledge."
(Hosea 4:6, KJV)

Your identity is shaped by what you believe,
And what you believe is shaped by what you **consume**.

If your inputs are full of fear, distortion, or shallow values,
Your inner world will reflect that noise.

That's why we must become **students of virtue**,
People who pursue excellence, truth, love and wisdom.

Chapter 2: Identity - Becoming Who We Really Are

In that season of my life, I would say
(Outside of the Holy Spirit) YouTube was my best friend.

I watched stories of restoration.
Interviews of people whose lives were turned around.
Testimonies that reminded me:
Even the darkest moments can be turned for good.

I began to limit interactions that pulled me away from purpose.
Some didn't understand why I no longer engaged in old patterns,
But I wasn't rejecting people.

I was refusing what was keeping me stuck.

What once looked like cycles
Was actually God doing quiet, careful work beneath the surface,
Bringing hidden flaws to light,
Weeding out distortion,
Reordering my habits,
Shaping how I carried myself, my home, and my atmosphere.

And even though I didn't do it perfectly,

As I removed distortion and renewed my inputs, even in small ways,
Something deeper was happening.
I was beginning (at heart) to *agree with truth.*
And that agreement was enough.

Enough to quiet the noise,
Enough to try,
Enough to believe that maybe the vision God placed in me
Was worth putting on paper.

Example:
Swapping passive scrolling for Scripture,

Trading entertainment for encouragement,
And replacing worldly noise with Kingdom culture.

It didn't just shift my mood, it shifted my mindset.

Reflect:
What am I allowing into my environment that's shaping how I live?

---

2. Write, Reveal and Surrender

There came a moment when God said,
"Write your life."

So I did.

Not my doubts,
But a vision.
A picture of my life at its highest level.

I wrote what I wanted to become.
What I hoped to create.
What I dreamed of doing,
Even if part of me thought it was too much, too far, or too bold.

I included everything.
Even things I once felt were silly, small, or out of reach.

I poured out private hopes,
Hidden desires,
Even the parts of me I'd never voiced before.

Example:
Some things I wrote felt awkward to admit,
But I trusted that if it was in me,
It was worth surrendering.

The good. The bad. The ugly.

Chapter 2: Identity - Becoming Who We Really Are

So I gave it to God.
Not to be dismissed,
But to be refined.

Reflect:
What vision have I buried because it felt "too much"?
Have I trusted God enough to carry it with me?

---

3. Struggle Well

Struggling well doesn't mean you've failed, it means you've chosen the harder, holier path: to be honest.

Honest with yourself.

Honest with God.

Honest about what you believe, even when what feels right seems to clash with what Scripture says is true.

To struggle well means not hiding in distraction or denial, but naming your doubts and bringing them into the light.

It means facing the thoughts that spiral, the fears that shake you, the questions that feel too big to ask.

The Israelites were taught this in the wilderness.

When deadly snakes struck them, God didn't take the snakes away,

He told them to look at one.
To stare at what hurt them,
To lift their eyes in faith,
And live.
(See Numbers 21:4–9)

It wasn't coping. It was transformation.

This Is Love, Not Religion

And interestingly, modern psychology backs this truth.
Studies have shown that when people face what they fear,
rather than suppress or avoid it, the brain begins to rewire itself.
This process, known as *fear extinction*, actually reduces anxiety over time.

It's as if science is catching up with what Scripture has always taught:
Healing begins with truth,
And freedom flows from facing what we fear in the presence of God.

Example:
I remember wrestling with fears I couldn't even name.
Instead of pretending they weren't there, I started praying them out loud,
Holding them before God.
And slowly, peace began to replace panic.
Not because I had all the answers,
But because I stopped hiding from the questions.

Reflect:
What fear or belief have I been avoiding?
What might happen if I choose to face it with God?

You don't have to fight for your identity.
You just have to make space for God to reveal it.

Before identity can be lived, it must be focused.
Mentally identify what you truly want,
Because whatever you fix your attention on
Will grow in your heart, soul, and mind.

For example,
When you cross the road, your goal is on getting to the other side,

Chapter 2: Identity - Becoming Who We Really Are

Your focus isn't on a lion in Africa.
Yet many of us allow our thoughts to wander
Into danger zones that have no bearing on our current walk.

Imagination is powerful, but it needs discernment.
Learning when to reject unaligned or unhealthy thoughts is part of maturity.

Track the *"why"* behind a thought,
Especially if it contradicts God's word.
And as you do, you begin to reclaim your inner narrative.

This life is like crossing a road.
Let your focus reflect where you truly want to go.

You are not the fruit-producer.
You are the garden-keeper.
Your role is to clear the ground, tend the soil and trust the Spirit.

Because when your habits start reflecting your values,
Your identity will no longer be borrowed,
It will be **embodied**.

You'll be a light to the nations.

But here's why this matters so much:
Not all versions of light are from God.

Sometimes, what glows is just a distraction,
A shadow disguised as revelation.

Let's talk about discernment,
And how to protect our identity when deception looks divine.

The Insidious Light: Discernment in the Age of Deception

Deception doesn't always look dark.
Sometimes it looks divine.

It comes clothed in opportunity,
But void of obedience.
Wrapped in affirmation,
But detached from alignment.

This is what Scripture means when it says:

"Satan himself masquerades as an angel of light."
(2 Corinthians 11:14, NIV)

Truth may shine differently depending on where you stand…

But light is not multiple just because its rays are many.

There is one sun. One Source. One Truth.

Not every light is from God.
Not every yes is heaven's invitation.
Not every platform is purpose.

In today's world, identity is often shaped by false light,
Messages that sound empowering, but are empty of truth.

You hear:
"Follow your heart."
"Do what feels right."
"Speak your truth."

But when your truth is shaped by trauma instead of truth,
It might feel familiar, but it won't be fruitful.

Because here's the hard truth:
The enemy doesn't need to convince you to serve him,
He just needs you to stop serving God.

Chapter 2: Identity - Becoming Who We Really Are

To detach your identity from your Creator
And connect it to counterfeit comfort.

He tempts with independence.
A version of identity that no longer requires intimacy.

Because if he can confuse your identity,
He doesn't have to fight your purpose.
A stolen sense of self keeps life on pause.

That's how deception works.
It flatters your wounds,
Magnifies your gifts,
And lures you into spiritual independence.

But discernment cuts through the noise.

Discernment says:
"Just because it works doesn't mean it's right."
"Just because it feels good doesn't mean it's God."

I've seen opportunities I could've taken,
That would've elevated me quickly,
But silently killed my character.

Discernment doesn't come from overthinking.
It comes from intimacy.

The more time you spend with God,
The easier it becomes to recognise when something is off,
Even if it looks like light.

When you know who you are,
You stop following every flicker.
You stop shape-shifting to fit in light that wasn't made for you.

Because when you carry truth on the inside,
You don't need to chase it on the outside.

Let's close this chapter and root it in what remains.

Closing Thoughts

In this chapter, we explored the truth that **identity is not something we create, it's something we uncover.**

Our true self is not defined by external opinions, past wounds, or performance.
It is **revealed through a relationship with the One who formed us.**

We encountered the Spirit of Knowledge,
Who doesn't just give information, He unveils insight.
He brings revelation that aligns our name, our nature and our narrative with heaven's intention.

We looked to **Day Two of creation**, where God separated the waters and established the heavens.
This division was not chaos, it was clarity.
Identity begins with divine distinction: not just who you are, but who you are not.

This is the process of identity: **Separation. Identification. Restoration.**

We reflected on Moses at the burning bush,
Where God responded to his insecurity with, *"I AM."*
Identity doesn't begin with our ability,
It begins with God's presence.

Next we saw I didn't find my identity by achieving more.
I found it when I laid down the script I wrote for myself.
In surrender, the Father rewrote what I believed,
Not just about life, but about me.

And we practiced the disciplines of shaping identity:
Creating an environment, speaking vision and protecting what's within.

Chapter 2: Identity - Becoming Who We Really Are

Not through striving, but through surrender,
Because your identity is most powerful when it's rooted in truth.

You are not who the world says you are.
You are who God says you are.

You are not your failures.
Not your fears.
Not your past.

You are seen.
Named.
Formed.
Known.

You don't have to find your identity,
You only have to agree with it.

Because the same God who separated the heavens
Has set you apart.

Not to perform,
But to **be**.

Now that you've discovered who you are,
It's time to let that truth **move**.

Next, we step into **Animation**,
Where identity becomes visible,

And your life begins to speak what your soul already knows.

RECLAIMING YOUR IDENTITY

If lost, please return to the bible and prayer

Prayer Decreeing Identity: Abiding in Who I Am

I am not who the world says I am,
I am who God says I am.

I am a child of the Most High *(John 1:12)*,
Fearfully and wonderfully made *(Psalm 139:14)*,
Created in His image *(Genesis 1:27)*,
And known before I was formed *(Jeremiah 1:5)*.

I am the righteousness of God in Christ Jesus *(2 Corinthians 5:21)*,
Not because of what I've done,
But because of what He has done for me.

Chapter 2: Identity - Becoming Who We Really Are

I am chosen, royal and set apart *(1 Peter 2:9)*.
I am seated with Christ in heavenly places *(Ephesians 2:6)*,
Not beneath, but above.

Shame and guilt have no place in me.
There is now no condemnation for those who are in Christ Jesus *(Romans 8:1)*.

I am deeply loved, fully accepted and eternally secure.
My identity is not fragile, it is founded.
Not shaped by people's opinions,
But rooted in God's truth.

I speak life over myself.
I walk in truth.
I abide in who I really am.

In Jesus' name.
Amen.

This Is Love, Not Religion

Chapter 3: Animation - Expressing Our True Self

"And God said, Let the waters under the heaven be gathered together unto one place, and let the dry land appear: and it was so. And God called the dry land Earth; and the gathering together of the waters called He Seas: and God saw that it was good... And the earth brought forth grass, and herb yielding seed after his kind, and the tree yielding fruit, whose seed was in itself... And the evening and the morning were the third day."
(Genesis 1:9–13, KJV)

What Is Animation?

Animation is not performance.
It is *expression*, truth in motion.

It's how your identity becomes visible.
Not just in words, but in how you move, live, love, and show up.
Animation isn't just in how you move.

This Is Love, Not Religion

It's in how you dress,
How you decorate,
How you choose what feels like home.
Your preferences.
Your style.
Even your quirks.

The way you sing in the kitchen.
The playlists that move your soul.
The colours you wear because they make you feel alive.

These aren't random.
They're sacred.

They are the quiet language of your identity,
Whispering truth without needing permission.

You're not performing.
You're expressing.
And when that expression flows from your core,
You're not just living.
You're animating.
Animation is the outer witness of an inner reality.

You're not acting, you're abiding.
You're not mimicking, you're manifesting.

When you are animated,
Your life reflects heaven's rhythm.

God doesn't rush this.
He unfolds it in layers, just like creation.

From dry land, He calls forth growth:

- **Grass**: Instinct. Raw movement. The courage to begin.
- **Herbs**: Personality. Sensitivity. Emotion shaped by grace.
- **Trees**: Maturity. Influence. A life that gives and bears fruit.

Chapter 3: Animation - Expressing Our True Self

This is the pattern:
You start by moving.
Then you grow.
Then you give.

Animation honours the process.
It is the journey of becoming visible.
Not for the sake of performance,
But for the sake of *purpose*.

When surrendered to God,
Your animation becomes worship.

The One who helps us walk this journey…
From movement to maturity is the **Spirit of Counsel**.

Let's explore how He doesn't just show us what's true,
But walks with us as we live it out.

The Rooted Spirit Manifested: The Spirit of Counsel

The *Spirit of Counsel* is not just a voice of advice…
He is the presence of wisdom *in motion*.

He doesn't just speak truth.
He walks with you through it.

He guides, but doesn't force.
He corrects, but doesn't condemn.
He shows the way and then teaches you how to walk in it.

This Spirit is personal.
Relational.
Practical.

This Is Love, Not Religion

He aligns your steps with heaven's intention,
And helps you respond to life with divine strategy,
Not just emotional reaction.

That's why the Spirit of Counsel is essential to animation.

Because animation isn't about impulsive movement.
It's about *guided* movement.

It's the difference between drifting and walking with purpose.
Between reacting to pain and responding to God.

The Spirit of Counsel whispers,

"This is the way, walk in it."
(Isaiah 30:21, NIV)

And in that whisper, clarity comes.

We often wait for a blueprint.
But He gives us a compass.

He doesn't just want to direct your behaviour.
He wants to develop your character,
So that every step reflects who you truly are.

We see this rhythm clearly on Day Three of creation,
A day of gathering, revealing, and calling forth.

It was the first time the earth *moved*...
And from that movement, life began to rise.

Let's look at how that moment in Genesis mirrors your becoming.

Chapter 3: Animation - Expressing Our True Self

Creation and the Third Day

"And God said, 'Let the water under the sky be gathered to one place, and let dry ground appear.' ... And there was evening and there was morning—the third day."
(Genesis 1:9–13, NIV)

First, He gathered the chaotic waters.
Then, land appeared, formed, but dry.

This moment is like a woman whose water breaks,
The beginning of birth.

What was once hidden is now ready to emerge.
What was forming in silence now cries to be seen.

The dry land didn't look fruitful at first.
But God still called it good,
Because He saw the *potential*.

This is what animation really is:
It's not just movement.
It's the *visible unfolding* of identity.

God doesn't just want you to know who you are,
He wants you to *express* it, *grow* in it, and *give* from it.

Animation is when your hidden truth becomes your visible life.

Not to perform,
But to produce according to your kind.

When your life feels like it's being pulled in different directions, ask yourself:

- What is God gathering?
- What dry ground is He trying to reveal beneath the surface?

Because growth doesn't begin with doing.
It begins with *being made visible*.

Because when you express what God planted in you,
He is glorified.

"And God saw that it was good."

And just like the dry land that emerged from hidden waters,
There comes a moment in every story
When what was forming in silence
Must begin to move in the open.

This is where animation becomes personal.

Because it's one thing to *know* who you are.
It's another thing to *let your life speak it.*

To act on what you've seen.
To carry what God has called forth in you.

Moses knew the tension.
He had identity,
But he hadn't yet found his expression.

Let's step into his story,
And see how God brought voice to the silence.

A Living Example: Moses Finds His Voice (Exodus 3–4)

Moses is a mirror of the animation journey.
He had identity, Hebrew by birth, Egyptian by upbringing,
But his expression was buried beneath fear, rejection, and silence.

After killing the Egyptian, he fled,

Chapter 3: Animation - Expressing Our True Self

Not just from Pharaoh, but from himself.

Then God met him at the burning bush,
And reignited not just his calling,
But his confidence.

"Now go; I will help you speak and will teach you what to say."
(Exodus 4:12, NIV)

Still, Moses hesitated. He argued.
He questioned his voice.
He pointed to his limitations.

"Pardon your servant, Lord. I have never been eloquent... I am slow of speech and tongue."
(Exodus 4:10, NIV)

He thought his quirks disqualified him,
But God didn't correct the stammer, He called through it.
Because animation isn't perfection,
It's permission.

God wasn't looking for a polished speaker,
He was looking for an honest vessel.

Moses preferred the background.
He didn't seek the spotlight,
But God still called his voice, his manner, his quiet way of leading.

And even his staff, the object he leaned on in daily life,
Became the sign of divine power.

Because God doesn't erase your personality to use you,
He breathes through it.

Moses became a leader not by charisma,
But by surrender,
By trusting that even his unpolished self

This Is Love, Not Religion

Could carry the weight of heaven's plan.

This is the core of animation:

Not performance,
Not mimicry,
But movement in the style of who you truly are.

And here's what's beautiful:

Because Moses honoured the boundary,
Agreed with his identity,
And yielded his unrefined instincts,
God was able to animate him in ways that defied nature.

A staff became a sign.
A sea split open.
Water flowed from a rock.

The miraculous didn't begin with performance,
It began with surrender.

The Scenario: When Identity Waits in Silence

You've spent time discovering who you are.
You've drawn boundaries. You've rooted your identity.

But now... everything feels quiet.

There's a deep truth inside of you, a knowing, a fire.

But your days feel muted.

You go to work. Sit through meetings. Engage in conversations.
And yet, your voice and your actions feel locked away.

Chapter 3: Animation - Expressing Our True Self

Your heart is speaking...
But your life isn't echoing it.

This is the ache of a life not yet **animated**.
A soul waiting for permission to move.
A truth waiting for a body to live in.
A calling still sitting in the silence.

I know that place.
I lived there.

And the shift didn't come through striving,
It came in a moment I didn't expect.

Let me take you there.
Back to a quiet town, a global lockdown,
And a heart on fire, waiting to breathe.

My Turning Point: The Release in Lockdown

1. The Revelation Within Confinement

I remember when I finally unearthed the truth about who I was,
But I was **unsure** how to express it.

In the early days of lockdown, I found myself in Chelmsford, UK.

God was revealing who He is,
And who I am.

I felt like a lion in a cage, roaring on the inside, pacing on the outside.

Lockdown, the irony.

2. The Urge to Express

I wanted to express.
I needed to create.

I started writing, drawing, creating,
Being a **visible version of the invisible God** in me.

3. The Boundaries of Birthing

But that birthing needed boundaries.
That power needed shaping.

So God gave me space.
Not just to be seen, but to be formed.

He protected others from me… and me from myself.
Because even good intentions can cause harm if they aren't refined.

4. Trusting the Process

I didn't want to stay stagnant out of fear.
I trusted that God would cover the process as I put my best foot forward,
Choosing love. Choosing kindness.

I wasn't perfect.
But many still saw light in me, **His light**.

Chapter 3: Animation - Expressing Our True Self

5. The Honest Awakening

Living honestly became the doorway.
Growing in truth became the key.
Faith was what helped me cross the threshold.

And in that moment, something came alive:

I realised that **animation** is the act of bringing your identity to life.

It's when your inner truth finally steps into the open.
Not to perform,
But to **bloom**.

---

6. The Intention to Bloom

But blooming doesn't happen by accident.
It takes intention.
It takes alignment.

Let's look at how to animate your life in real time,
With your heart, your soul, your mind and your movement.

Practicing Animation in Real Life

Animation isn't accidental, it's intentional.
If identity is who you are, then animation is how you live it out,
In how you move, speak and show up in the world.

But how do you know *what* to practice?
God made it clear, not just once, but again and again:

This Is Love, Not Religion

"Love the Lord your God with all your heart, with all your soul, with all your strength." (Deuteronomy 6:5, NIV)

"And with all your mind." (Luke 10:27, NIV)

This is not a suggestion.
It's a **rhythm**, a divine alignment.
Heart.
Soul.
Mind.
Strength.

These aren't just inner parts of you.
They're **pathways of expression**.
They teach you how to love God in real time.
Not just with belief, but with embodiment.

So if you want to animate your identity,
Start by loving God in the way He designed you:
Fully.
Wholly.
Daily.

Here are four dimensions of animation, rooted in love, integrity and spiritual flow:

Heart: Abide in Love's Standard

Love is a standard. A foundation. A rock.

Feelings come alive from our love.
And God's love has a standard.

He is faithful despite how He feels.

That standard is revealed in Scripture
And made visible when we meditate on **how God moves**.

Chapter 3: Animation - Expressing Our True Self

A heart without the guide rails of truth spirals into chaos.

A heart that aligns with His standard becomes a safer container for divine expression.

Guard your heart *(Proverbs 4:23)*.
Let God's way of love define how you respond, how you lead and how you give.

But here's how we often fall away from love's true standards:

- **Trip**: When you recognise a lie and begin looking into its ways
- **Stumble**: When you entertain that lie by practising its preaching
- **Fall**: When you live that lie, convinced it's a good way

Love doesn't just need to be felt, it must be followed. And following it requires clarity about what is not love, even when it feels familiar.

How I practiced it:
It began with vulnerable intimacy.
I took time to get to know God.
Not just in theory, but in real life.
I looked for what He was doing,
How He did it,
And why.

I started asking questions.
And He started answering,
Through dreams,
Through patterns,
Through quiet signs hidden in my days.

There were moments when I prayed,
Not because I felt holy,
But because I realised my heart wasn't right.
I was scared to ask God to change me,
Because I knew He would respond.

This Is Love, Not Religion

And when He did,
It usually came with discomfort.
But that's often the mark of real growth.

Every year on my birthday,
I reflect on His work in my heart.
And while the outer fruit may not always be where I hope,
The inner transformation has been undeniable.
And that, for me, is the true reward.

From the inside out,
I want to be me.

I remember seeing teammates in America
Who needed weed to be themselves on the court.
They were outstanding too.
But I thought,
That can't be me.

I didn't want a version of myself
That relied on substances to show up.
I wanted to be outstanding in all areas,
Free in the heart,
And into how I animate.

Example:
Before speaking in a heated moment, you pause and ask,
"Is this how love moves?"
You choose patience instead of impulse, truth instead of ego.

Soul: Tune to a Clear Frequency

Your soul reflects what it consumes.
If you tune into distortion, you embody confusion.
If you pour in purity, clarity begins to flow.

Chapter 3: Animation - Expressing Our True Self

What you hear, watch, read and allow into your space
Shapes the **frequency** of your inner life.

Choose music, shows, books and input that mirror God's purity.
As you guard your soul, your flow will become more aligned.

How I Practiced It:
I started to see the soul as a river,
Transparent, flowing, longing.

Even when I was young,
I noticed how music could move me.
It didn't just entertain,
It shaped my appetite.
What I heard shifted my mood and emotion.
I wanted more of what I consumed.

And it wasn't just music.
Any gateway to my soul had the same effect.
What flowed in through my
Eyes, ears, nose and touch
Would shape what flowed out through my
Mind, mouth and action.

Like a river, things needed to be washed away.
And that required intention,
Patience, persistence, and grace.

Though difficult at times,
Boundaries became my rescue rope.
I began to agree less with what distorted me,
And more with what healed me.

God has given us great authority.
One simple click on a device
Can determine the realm we're aligning with.
And in that click, we may agree with:
Gossip. Hostility. Rage.
The world packages it as normal,
And sells it as culture.

This Is Love, Not Religion

But as God worked in my heart,
My soul began to whisper for more life.
So I learned to shift conversations,
To quiet the noise,
To shun what was wicked to my eyes.

Not perfectly,
But faithfully.
And I can say now,
I'm not who I used to be.
I'm better.
I'm freer.

I want to be like Job:
"*Blameless and upright, one who feared God and turned away from evil.*" (Job 1:1, ESV)

So I began to pray:
"*Teach me to love what You love, and hate what You hate.*" (Psalm 100:4, NIV)

For ourselves to be who we are expressively,
Our souls must be stripped from the junk that pollutes our being.

Example:
You replace a playlist full of aggression and lust
With worship, instrumental, or truth-filled lyrics.
Over time, you notice the shift, your mood, thoughts and even tone begin to change.

Mind: Practise Presence

The present mind is where clarity grows.
When you're fully here, mentally engaged, emotionally aware,
You become a vessel of peace, not pressure.

Chapter 3: Animation - Expressing Our True Self

A present mind makes space for divine awareness.

Fix your thoughts on what is pure, noble and true *(Philippians 4:8).*
Silence distraction. Return to centre. Choose stillness over speed.

How I Practiced It:
When God told me *"patience,"*
He set my life to learn just that.
He didn't rush me.
He slowed me.
He taught me how to be still.

Through patience, I began to notice:
Stillness produces awareness.
Awareness nurtures understanding.
Understanding builds care.
Care leads to wisdom.
Wisdom makes space for mistakes.
Mistakes refine your perseverance.
And perseverance matures into love.

I realised,
If heaven is outside of time,
It must be a place of constant present presence.
And if we are to bring heaven to earth,
Shouldn't we practice being present too?

This doesn't mean we neglect the future,
Or deny our past.
It means we learn to live from a place of trust,
Trusting God's power.
Trusting His timing.
Trusting His love.

Being present frees the mind.
Because anxiety tries to grip the future,
To understand, control, protect.
It often masks fear in the clothing of planning.

This Is Love, Not Religion

It wants life to unfold on terms we can handle.

People.
Problems.
Purpose.
All placed in boxes we feel safe with.

But the Lord says:
"Trust in the Lord with all your heart, and lean not on your own understanding;
In all your ways acknowledge Him, and He will make your paths straight." (Proverbs 3:5–6, NIV)

And then there's depression,
Often tethered to the past, or within.
It whispers despair.
It dims our interest.
It suffocates joy.

Depression is not always disconnection from God,
But sometimes from the part of Him
That reminds you who you are.
The part that says:
"You are not alone."
It forgets to:
"Enter His gates with thanksgiving and His courts with praise." (Psalm 100:4)

It is a darkness
That cannot comprehend the Light. *(John 1:5)*

Anxiety reaches too far forward.
Depression withdraws too far within.
Neither lives fully in the now.
And growth cannot happen
Outside of the present moment.

Being aware is tending your life like a garden.
Yes, prepare for the seasons,

Chapter 3: Animation - Expressing Our True Self

But water what's here.
Today's soil.
Today's sun.

Where anxiety floods the field,
And depression leaves it dry,
Presence speaks:
"This is enough for today,
And God has me."

Emotionally, this means letting your mind flow,
As thoughts pass through,
Notice them.
Where did they come from?
Where are they going?

Your thoughts are not always you.
Measure them by the Word.
Cast down what isn't true.
Anchor what is in hope.
All in alignment with God's voice.

By doing this,
You'll begin to accept the stage you're in,
Not with shame, but with clarity.
You'll become aware of what's happening within,
And join it to the hope of what you're becoming.
Not rushing ahead,
Not judging the pace,
But appreciating where you are,
With faith in where you're going.

And in all this,
You'll begin to discover joy in the process.
There will still be days of struggle,
Moments when your mind wrestles to transform.
But don't let go.
Hold on to hope.
And remember:

You are doing the best you can,
And God is doing the rest.

Example:
You start the day with breath and Scripture instead of your phone.
That simple act slows your pace and sharpens your mind.
You move through your day anchored, not scattered.

Action: Be in Your Way

Your actions are an overflow of your inner formation.
When your heart is grounded in love,
Your behaviour naturally begins to follow.

You become more **sensitive** to what's in alignment with God's way of being.

Let your movement reflect your convictions.
Allow your decisions to come from discernment, not distraction.

How I Practiced It:
The actions we take
Are like seeds we plant for the person we are becoming.
But becoming isn't perfect,
It's progressive.
And grace meets us in the gaps.
As it is written:
"Though the righteous fall seven times, they rise again."
(Proverbs 24:16, NIV)

That verse gave me freedom to fail,
To fall forward
And get up wiser.

But rising wasn't just about effort,

Chapter 3: Animation - Expressing Our True Self

It required alignment.
If I wanted my steps to reflect heaven,
I had to agree with its process.
Grass. Herb. Tree.

Born into a world of sin,
I needed honesty.
Sometimes my feelings didn't match Scripture.
My impulses didn't always reflect truth.
But that wasn't cause for panic,
It was an invitation.
An invitation to pause,
To be still,
And let Christ recalibrate my soul.

As I surrendered,
My actions became less about performance,
And more about partnership.
God began stripping the dead weight,
The fear of opinions,
The pressure to please,
The need to perform.

And as I moved,
I discovered more of who I truly am.
Not less.

But I had to ask:
Why do I like this?
Where did I learn that?
What does Jesus say about it?

True action is born from true values.
I remember learning about Maslow's hierarchy of needs.
At one point in my life,
I lacked shelter, stability and community.
Yet strangely,
I was more whole than ever.
That pyramid,

This Is Love, Not Religion

It felt upside down.

I realised:
Self-actualisation didn't come last for me.
It came first,
Because Christ came first.

And then I remembered:
"Seek first the kingdom of God and His righteousness,
And all these things shall be added unto you."
(Matthew 6:33, NIV)

With that alignment,
My actions changed.
Not from effort,
But from overflow.

I saw the fruit of the Spirit take root.
Love.
Peace.
Faithfulness.
I moved differently.
I became confident in Christ within me.

And because I trusted the One within,
I finally trusted myself…
To simply be myself.

Example:
You're invited to say yes to something that sounds good, but doesn't feel right.
Instead of acting out of pressure, you pause.
You listen.
And you choose peace over performance.

Chapter 3: Animation - Expressing Our True Self

ANIMATE YOUR IDENTITY

Love the Lord your God with all...

Divine Progression

The Kingdom of God is not built on hustle, it flows in rhythm:

"The Kingdom of God is righteousness, peace and joy in the Holy Spirit."
(Romans 14:17, NIV)

It begins with a **righteous humbled heart**,
A heart aligned with truth.
That brings **peace** to your soul and mind.
And from that peace flows authentic **joy**,
Not from performance, but from presence.

This is animation:
Righteousness that moves.
Peace that expresses.
Joy that lives.

Because when your life moves in rhythm with heaven,
You don't have to force expression,
You just let what's real inside finally breathe.

Let's gather this all in.
And close with clarity.

Closing Thoughts

In this chapter, we discovered that **animation is the visible expression of our invisible identity**.

It's not performance, it's alignment.
It's how truth moves through your life.
You are not made to mimic, you are made to **manifest**.

Chapter 3: Animation - Expressing Our True Self

We explored the role of the **Spirit of Counsel**,
Who doesn't just tell us the truth, He walks with us through it.
He helps us respond to life with strategy, not just reaction.
He aligns our pace with heaven's plan.

We studied **Day Three of creation**, where God gathered the waters, revealed the land and called forth life: first grass, then herbs, then trees.
This is a blueprint for your own growth:
You move, you mature and then you give.

We examined Moses' journey:
How his voice was buried in fear,
And how God reignited his calling by helping him move from silence to legacy.

We looked at how the deepest movement often begins in stillness.

In confinement, I found clarity,

Not by striving, but by surrendering to the truth within.

That's when animation began: quiet, honest, alive.

And we practiced what it means to animate in real life,
Governing our heart, soul, mind and actions
So that our whole life flows in rhythm with God's love.

Animation is not about doing more,
It's about being **seen** rightly.

It's the courage to let who you are
Take up space without apology.

You're not made to hide your light,
You're made to reflect His.

This is not noise.
This is not performance.

This Is Love, Not Religion

This is your identity in motion.
Your truth in rhythm.
Your worship in movement.

When you express from love,
Resonate with truth,
Remain present in thought,
And move with integrity,

Your life becomes a living echo of heaven.

But movement alone isn't enough.
Without structure, even truth can become scattered.

Now it's time to learn how to **tend what you've brought to life**.

In the next chapter, we enter **Management**,
Where rhythms are established,
And what was expressed is now sustained.

Prayer Decreeing Animation: Breathing with You

I am not made to perform,
I am made to express the image of God within me.

I am fearfully and wonderfully made *(Psalm 139:14)*,
Created in His likeness to move in rhythm with heaven *(Genesis 1:26)*.
My identity is not a secret,
It's a seed that God is bringing to life.

I am filled with the Spirit of Counsel *(Isaiah 11:2)*,
Who leads me in wisdom, clarity and divine flow.
I do not drift, I walk with purpose.
I do not react, I respond with grace.

My heart is aligned with love.
My soul is tuned to truth.

Chapter 3: Animation - Expressing Our True Self

My mind is present and at peace.
My actions flow from righteousness, not restlessness.

The Kingdom of God lives in me,
Righteousness, peace and joy in the Holy Spirit *(Romans 14:17)*.
This is my rhythm.
This is my witness.
This is my worship.

I don't just exist, I express.
I don't just move, I manifest what's been planted.

My life is not random.
It is a visible reflection of God's invisible design.

In Jesus' name.
Amen.

This Is Love, Not Religion

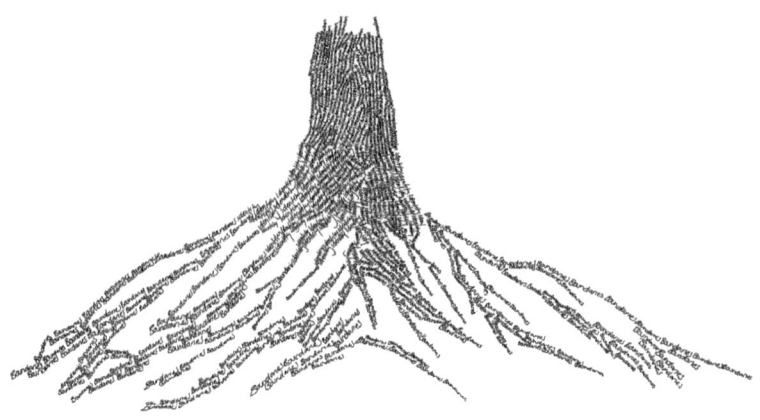

Chapter 4: Management - Bringing Order from Chaos

"And God said, Let there be lights in the firmament of the heaven to divide the day from the night; and let them be for signs, and for seasons, and for days, and years: And let them be for lights in the firmament of the heaven to give light upon the earth: and it was so... And God saw that it was good. And the evening and the morning were the fourth day."
(Genesis 1:14–19, KJV)

What Is Management?

Management is not about control...
It's about *alignment*.

It's the intentional realisation of your God-given animation.
It turns passion into pace.
It turns vision into rhythm.
It turns what was stirred into something *sustained*.

This Is Love, Not Religion

Management doesn't just organise your life,
It orders your soul.

It ensures your energy, time, and resources don't scatter,
But multiply with meaning.

Management is built in us, and it rests on us.

Even the care of our bodies, trimming hair, cleaning teeth, washing skin, is a form of stewardship.

It's a small echo of Eden's call: to subdue, to tend, to bring order.

Not out of vanity, but care.

Not just hygiene, but holiness.

Because management starts with the body you wake up in,

A reminder that what is governed well, grows well.

From a biblical view, management is a form of *worship*.
To steward what God entrusts
Is to mirror His nature,
The Sustainer. The Order-Giver. The Rhythm-Setter.

From a practical view, management is freedom.
It frees you from chaos, distraction, and exhaustion.
It teaches you to move with *pace*... Not pressure.

Whether you're managing a business, a ministry, a household,
Or simply your own inner world,
The principle remains:

What you don't manage will manage you.
But what you tend with intention will multiply with grace.

Chapter 4: Management - Bringing Order from Chaos

And the Spirit that makes management sacred,
That turns systems into worship and rhythms into revelation...
The **Spirit of Understanding**.

Let's explore how this Spirit helps us not just receive God's word,
But *arrange* our lives in step with it.

The Rooted Spirit Manifested: The Spirit of Understanding

The *Spirit of Understanding* is more than mental clarity,
It is a supernatural ability to grasp the *meaning* and *significance* of God's truth.

It is the Holy Spirit interpreting divine intention,
And imparting that insight into your spirit
So that you don't just know what is true,
You live in *agreement* with it.

Understanding bridges the gap between knowledge and wisdom.
It connects what is taught to what is lived.
It reveals how to walk in righteousness,
Not just in principle,
But in *practice*.

This Spirit helps you discern:

- What matters?
- What belongs where?
- How do I live this out faithfully, sustainably, and well?

We see it in creation.
We see it in instruction.
We see it in how Jesus lived,
With *pace*, *presence*, and *power*.

Never hurried.
Never reactive.
Always ordered from within.

We see this divine structure clearly on Day Four of creation.

Not a new material.
Not a louder move.
But an *arrangement*.
The sun, the moon, the stars, set in place
To govern time, rhythm, and direction.

Let's explore how these lights weren't just celestial, they were *strategic*.
A divine pattern for how we manage everything entrusted to us.

Creation and the Fourth Day

"And God said, 'Let there be lights in the vault of the sky to separate the day from the night… and let them serve as signs to mark sacred times, and days, and years.'" (Genesis 1:14–19, NIV)

On Day One, God separated light from darkness.
He established the boundaries of time, space, and matter.

But on Day Four,
He filled that space with *order*.

Sun. Moon. Stars.
Placed not for decoration,
But for *governance*.

This is the turning point of creation:
God didn't add more matter,
He gave movement its meaning.

Chapter 4: Management - Bringing Order from Chaos

- The sun ruled the day.
- The moon ruled the night.
- The stars held positions of purpose.

Each light carried not just brilliance,
But *assignment*.

Management in God's design is not about shining louder,
It's about shining *with purpose*.

And this is the Spirit of Understanding at work: Revealing how to govern what God has formed, so that life can flourish, not fragment.

Understanding Divine Management: A Picture of Light

A friend once asked me,

"How can science say the sun came before the earth, when the Bible clearly shows God created the earth first?"

They trusted the Word,
But this part didn't fully make sense.

So I prayed.
And what came to mind was simple: A television… and a remote.

I said:

"Imagine I'm watching TV. I use the remote to change the channel. Then I hand the remote to someone else. The image is still on the screen, but someone new is managing it. That's what God did: He gave light first, because He is light. Later, He created the sun, moon, and stars to manage that light."

This Is Love, Not Religion

The sun isn't the source.
It's a *steward*.

Like a manager takes care of something the owner created.

Then my friend added:

"You know, a bird can knock the antenna off a TV, just like the enemy tries to knock us off our connection with God."

That struck me.

When the antenna is disconnected, the image goes fuzzy.

It's the same in the Spirit: When we lose *connection*, we lose *clarity*.

And when the image is off,
The way we manage life becomes distorted.

The sun, moon, and stars each manage light,
But only when they're *aligned* with the Creator's intention.

The same goes for us.

Managing anything in God's image and likeness
Must be done with *reverence*.

Whether you're carrying light in the heavens,
Or a calling on earth,
You're called to manage it well.

Just like a screen reflects a signal,
We reflect the One who made us.

And if we want to carry the light well,
We must remain connected to the *Source*.

Chapter 4: Management - Bringing Order from Chaos

Because what was set in motion wasn't random,
Each light was placed to govern with purpose:

Signs: Divine signals and spiritual invitations
Not coincidences, but heaven's cues.
Moments that prompt us to move, pause, pray, or prepare.

Seasons: Purposeful phases: preparation, growth, fruition, rest
Every phase is sacred.
Each one forms what the next will need.

Days: The present moment: daily obedience and rhythm
Where truth meets habit.
Where consistency becomes worship.

Years: Long-term development and legacy
Time reveals what's been rooted.
God's promises unfold over generations.

The Sun: Identity and Authority
The sun rules the day.
It represents Christ, the unshakable Light.
A picture of divine presence and leadership.
True management begins with being anchored in who you are.

The Moon: Reflection and Rhythm
The moon holds no light of its own.
It reflects the sun, just as we reflect God's wisdom through humility and rhythm.
Its waxing and waning teach us to honour process, embrace rest, and move in time.

The Stars: Vision and Multiplication
The stars mark direction and promise.
Each placed with intention, like disciplines that shape our character and legacy.
They guide through darkness, one light at a time.

This isn't just ancient poetry,
It's a *heavenly system*.

This Is Love, Not Religion

A divine framework for how we manage what God entrusts.

A Living Example: Moses organises the People *(Exodus 18)*

Moses was a man of miracles,
But miracles alone couldn't sustain a nation.

After the Red Sea parted,
After the manna fell,
After water flowed from the rock,
Moses was still exhausted.

Not from lack of power,
But from a lack of *management*.

He was doing everything himself: Settling disputes. Hearing concerns.
Guiding the people, while burning out in the process.

Then came Jethro.
A father-in-law, yes.
But also a divine interruption.

"What you are doing is not good…
You will surely wear yourself out,
Both you and these people with you."
(Exodus 18:17–18, NRSV)

Jethro didn't question the *calling*,
He challenged the *system*.

Because calling without structure
Will eventually collapse.

Chapter 4: Management - Bringing Order from Chaos

So he gave Moses a blueprint:

- Appoint capable, trustworthy leaders.
- Delegate responsibility.
- Handle only what belongs in your hands.

And Moses listened.
He didn't defend his pace,
He adjusted it.

That's maturity.
That's the Spirit of Understanding in action.

Because even holy work requires holy rhythm.
Even sacred assignments need structure to survive.

God had already delivered Israel,
But He needed Moses to *govern* what had been given.

This was Day Four in motion: The shift from miracle to maintenance.
From pressure to pattern.
From fire to framework.

We often celebrate the breakthrough,
But overlook the wisdom that follows.

Because movement alone can't carry a mission.
Without structure, even the anointed get exhausted.

Moses didn't need more energy,
He needed divine *strategy*.

And just like Moses,
We are not called to carry everything.
We are called to manage what's ours,
And release what's not.

But what happens when you don't have that system yet?

This Is Love, Not Religion

What happens when your purpose is active,
Your gifting is stirring,
But your pace is unsustainable?

This is the tension many face:
When movement begins to outpace management,
And what once felt purposeful now feels overwhelming.

Let's talk about that space.
Because even holy momentum can lead to burnout
If it's not brought into order.

The Scenario: When Passion Turns to Pressure

There comes a moment when everything feels like it's moving,
But not everything feels manageable.

You're doing the work.
Saying yes to purpose.
You've stepped into the flow.
But under the surface... something feels off.

You're tired.
Not just physically, but **spiritually scattered**.

Your calendar is full, but your soul feels thin.
Your gifting is active, but your systems are weak.
And your desire to honour God is genuine,
But your rhythm is unsustainable.

This is what it looks like when **movement outpaces management**.

You know what matters.
But you're too worn out to give it the attention it deserves.

Chapter 4: Management - Bringing Order from Chaos

Your identity is clear.
Your purpose is alive.
But your habits...
Your schedule...
Your boundaries...

They're not holding it together.

And here's the hidden truth:

It's possible to be full of purpose
And still feel **disorganised** on the inside.

It's possible to look fruitful,
But be slowly breaking beneath the surface
Because there's no structure to sustain what God has begun.

This is why God introduces rhythm.
This is why Day Four comes **before** dominion on Day Six.

Because **God doesn't just want you to move**,
He wants you to **last**.

And what carries you forward
Is not just calling.
It's **consistency**.
It's knowing when to say yes.
When to rest.
When to recalibrate.

That's what management is for:
To protect what matters most
So your life doesn't collapse under its own potential.

I've lived in that tension.

I knew what I carried.
I had vision, insight and fire in my bones,
But I was slowly burning out in the name of purpose.

Let me show you how grace taught me to breathe again.
And how management became a gift, not a burden.

My Turning Point: Learning to Tend What God Gave Me

1. Mistaking Zeal for Maturity

There was a time I mistook zeal for maturity.
If I was excited, I thought I was ready.

I launched quickly.
Shared widely.
Committed often.

But I didn't have the rhythms to sustain what I'd started.
I was a starter,
Not yet a steward.
And that gap led to burnout…
And too many unfinished assignments.

---

2. The Message That Changed Everything

Then came a season of deep internal growth.
In that space, I came across a message by Dr. Myles Munroe,
A teaching on Kingdom management.
He shared:
God owns everything. We're entrusted to reflect Him through how we manage.

That struck me.
Just like the moon reflects the sun,
I was made to reflect His **order**, not just His **energy**.

That shift set me free.
Free from control.
Free from anxiety.
Free from the pressure to make everything happen on my own.

---

3. The Pivot Away from Worry

And before that time, I read Matthew 6:25–34,
Jesus' invitation not to worry.
And I responded, simply and honestly:

"I will not worry anymore."

That wasn't just a prayer.
It was a pivot.

I started trusting God with the weight of my future.
I stopped grasping and started **stewarding**.
Not forcing, just being faithful.

---

4. Becoming a Steward

He taught me to manage not just my potential,
But the unrefined parts of me, too.
And to extend that grace to others.

It wasn't easy.
I didn't grow up in a large family.
I didn't always know how to love well.
But slowly, God began to rewrite my patterns,
Turning me from selfish tendencies,
And breaking habits I didn't even know I had.

5. Interdependence by Design

That's when I saw it clearly:

People need people.

We weren't designed to operate in isolation.
We were created for **holy interdependence**,
First with God,
Then with one another.

Each of us carries something unique.
Some love to build.
Some love to support.
Some teach. Others nurture.
Some organise. Others initiate.

And when we all move in our divine design,
We create space for others to do the same.

---

6. The Sacredness of Serving

If you like to cook, clean, plan, encourage, or strategise,
Don't minimise your gift.

Use it.
Serve with it.
Because real management isn't just about things,
It's about ecosystems. Relationships. Assignments.
It's about cultivating what enables others to flourish.

7. The Reward of Tending

I kept showing up.
Kept tending what God gave me.
Kept my garden.

And one day, it hit me:

God doesn't just bless movement.
He blesses management.

He honours what is tended with care.
He multiplies what is cultivated with consistency.
And sometimes…
He teaches you that lesson in the most unexpected ways.

---

8. A Lesson in Obedience

I remember one such moment like it happened yesterday.

I was in Texas, in a city known for its crime.
At the time, I was working in business sales,
Managing, grinding, growing.

One night as I got home, I heard it deep within:

"Don't lock your door."

It sounded absurd. But I obeyed.

That night, a friend called.

"I'm outside your door. Can I come in for the car keys?"
I told him, *"Yeah, it's already open."*

It was strange… but I didn't overthink it.

The next night, the same thing:
"Leave the door open."

Again, I obeyed. This time though.

My phone was on silent…

I woke up and immediately after my phone lit up,

God woke me up to see my incoming call.

And again, the same friend arrived, this time between 1 and 3 AM.
He needed the keys again.
The door was open.

---

9. God's Management Beyond Our Reach

Simple. But something in me shifted.

I realised:
God was managing my life at a level I couldn't even perceive.
He had aligned the **seconds** of my night
To meet someone else's need
Before I even knew it would happen.

He was showing me:
**Management isn't about what you control.
It's about what you surrender.**

It's trusting that the God who placed the stars
Can also schedule your steps.

That He doesn't just manage galaxies,
He manages **moments**.

And when you manage what's in your hands,
He will manage what's beyond your reach.

Chapter 4: Management - Bringing Order from Chaos

He will do the best He can for us,
As we do the best we can for Him.

---

10. The Real Question of Stewardship

So how do you steward the life God has entrusted to you?

How do you bring order to what's already been formed,
And make space for purpose to flourish?

Let's get practical.
Let's learn how to **manage what matters**.

But there's more to managing than calendars and keys.
It's not just about movement,
It's about motive.
It's not just about doing things for God,
It's about doing them with Him.

God wasn't just helping me run life better,
He was calling me to mirror His nature.
And that call had been there from the beginning.
Hidden in the first garden, waiting to be remembered.

To Dress and Keep: A Deeper Mandate

Your flesh will always crave what is easy, immediate, and indulgent.

But your desires were never meant to be led by appetite,
They were made to be led by God.
To be washed.
To be refined.
To be fulfilled in His way and time.

Desires, left unchecked, are emotional, dangerous,

This Is Love, Not Religion

And easily influenced by the world's systems.
But truth, God's truth, the foundation.
It helps us measure desire against righteousness.

In Genesis 2:15, Adam was placed in the garden
"to dress it and to keep it."
To 'abad, to serve, to work.
To shamar, to guard, to protect.
Both are sacred.
Both are needed.

To dress is to serve God first,
Then the earth He entrusted to us:
Our bodies, our brothers,
Even creation itself.

To keep is to hedge,
To set a boundary,
Like a thorny wall encircling what is holy.
A life that protects what God calls sacred.

But Adam did not keep the garden from the serpent.
He failed to guard what was holy.
Instead, he served his flesh with the fruit,
Choosing desire over obedience,
Pride over trust.

And when he failed to protect what was entrusted,
All of humanity bore the consequence.

Genesis 4 reveals the same pattern.
Cain brought some fruit
Not the first,
Not the best.
It was the first sign that faith was missing.

Abel offered blood,
But it wasn't the blood that made it holy,
It was the belief behind it.

Chapter 4: Management - Bringing Order from Chaos

Faith made it pleasing.

Cain cultivated the earth,
But let jealousy grow in his heart.
He guarded the field,
But not human life.
And in that failure,
We see the distortion of both 'abad and shamar.

If pride leads your head, death will follow,
Because whatever rules your mind,
You'll end up serving with your life.

So what does that mean for us?

To serve is not just to perform.
It's to selflessly honour God,
So that His glory is revealed.

To keep is not just to control.
It's to stand as a guardian
Over the lives, hearts, and truths entrusted to us.

We are called to do both.
To dress and to keep.
To serve and to protect.
To love in action and guard in truth.

This is what Jesus fulfilled:
The Guardian with the thorny crown.
The Servant with pierced hands and feet.
He kept the covenant.
He served it with His life.

The Crown of Thorns, Shamar
He wore the guarding hedge,
Taking upon Himself the curse of thorns and thistles *(Genesis 3:18)*.

This Is Love, Not Religion

He didn't just protect life, He laid down His own to preserve ours.

The Pierced Hands and Feet, 'Abad
These were the instruments of His labour of love.
Not just a sacrifice, but a service.
He served the will of the Father unto death, so we could live.

And knowing in that moment His calling,
The salvation of humanity,
He embraced obedience,
He honoured the timing,
He fulfilled the purpose.
And He said:
"It is finished." *(John 19:30, NIV)*

Becoming > Goals

Don't Set Goals, Set Outcomes for Who You Want to Become.
The right virtues seen in the way of God
Help us see value in the way He sees.
And by that vision,
We learn to walk in the way we ought to.

One of the deepest sources of anxiety
Is how we frame progress.

Hear me clearly:
We often set goals, deadlines, achievements, metrics,
But the Kingdom is not built on ambition.
It's built on alignment.

If the Kingdom is about the King
Having His outcome in your life,
Then the question becomes:
Where should your focus be?

Not on goals that generate pressure,

Chapter 4: Management - Bringing Order from Chaos

But on outcomes that are rooted in virtue.

Let the outcomes you desire
Grow from the soil of Christlike character.
Let love shape your leadership.
Let patience shape your parenting.
Let truth shape your business.
Let gentleness govern your body.

When your outcomes are aligned with the image of Christ,
You'll begin to see His Kingdom unfold
In every area of life.

You'll stop chasing achievement
And start cultivating fruit.
You'll stop striving for control
And start stewarding what matters.

Because when your focus is virtue,
Worry loses its grip.
And goals no longer haunt you with *"not yet."*
They bow to the beauty of becoming.

Take this for example:
Two people want to get in shape.

The first sets a goal:
"I need to lose 10kg in 2 months."
They begin with strict discipline,
Tracking calories. Weighing food. Watching the scale.
At first, they feel powerful.
But underneath that intensity…
Anxiety grows.

What if the number doesn't drop?
What if progress slows?
What if people notice they're not "there" yet?

And even if they succeed,

This Is Love, Not Religion

The success is fragile, built on fear of failure.
Their worth becomes tied to performance.
Their pride whispers, "I did this."
And when life interrupts the plan,
They either spiral or self-punish.

They reached a goal,
But they didn't grow in character.
They became slimmer, maybe,
But not stronger in soul.

Their goal fed their ego,
But starved their peace.

Now look at the second person.

They set an outcome:
"I want to become someone who honours my body with care and discipline."

Their pace is different.
Less frantic.
More faithful.

They walk. They stretch. They nourish.
They fall short some days, but they return.
They learn to forgive themselves.
They start listening to their body, not punishing it.
They become patient with their process.
They begin making decisions out of honour, not haste.

And something holy happens:

Their body changes, yes.
But so does their being.

They become more thoughtful.
More joyful.
More grounded.

Chapter 4: Management - Bringing Order from Chaos

More gracious with others.
Because they've learned to be gracious with themselves.

Their outcome isn't just physical,
It's spiritual.
They're not chasing a number,
They're being formed into someone whole.

Because setting plans for God's glory
Is never just about what gets done,
It's about who you've become,
And how the situation you touched now reflects His presence.

And here's the deeper truth:

God is persistent and consistent.
He never fails.
He lovingly manages and adjusts our lives according to His will.
He is the same yesterday, today, and forever. *(Hebrews 13:8)*

We're not called to imitate His consistency in perfection,
But to mirror His faithfulness in our persistence.

They don't need to be consistent.
They just need to be persistent.

Consistency vs Persistence

The Bible says:
"Though the righteous fall seven times, they rise again..."
(Proverbs 24:16, NIV)

It doesn't say they never fall.
It says they rise.
Over and over.

Their righteousness isn't in perfection,
It's in returning.

That's persistence.

Consistency is like a clock,
Precise. Measured. Perfectly timed.

Persistence is like a heartbeat,
Sometimes fast, sometimes slow…
But always returning.
Always alive.

One is mechanical.
The other is miraculous.

God doesn't expect you to move like a machine.
He calls you to keep coming back like a son.
To return to the vine.
To rise again with grace.
To tend what He gave you, even if you dropped it yesterday.

Practicing Management in Daily Life

Management is not about control, it's about **alignment**.

To live wisely and sustainably, you need more than inspiration.
You need rhythm.
You need **Priority. Order. Discipline**, God's blueprint for fruitful stewardship.

In the next seven areas of your life,
We'll apply the P.O.D. System to show you how to create space for lasting fruit,
The kind that grows in season and sustains others beyond yourself.

Chapter 4: Management - Bringing Order from Chaos

1. Godliness: Governing Your Devotion

Priority:
"Seek first the kingdom of God and His righteousness…"
(Matthew 6:33, NIV)
Make vulnerability with God your non-negotiable starting point.

Order:
Set a clear routine for spiritual practice, daily time in the Word, worship, prayer.

Discipline:
Show up even when it's quiet. Stay rooted even when you don't feel it.

Example*:*
You begin each day by inviting God into your schedule.
You pause at midpoints to re-centre.
You don't just talk about devotion, you build it into your reality.

2. Mindset: Governing Your Thought Life

Priority:
Renew your mind by making God's truth the foundation of your thinking.
"Be transformed by the renewing of your mind…" (Romans 12:2, NIV)

Order:
Curate what you consume. Guard your mind from confusion and fear.

Discipline:
Take thoughts captive. Replace inner chatter with biblical affirmations.

Example:
You make a habit of declaring Scripture over yourself when doubt creeps in.
You replace toxic media with uplifting, truth-filled inputs.

---

3. Well-being: Governing Your Body

Priority:
Your body is a temple, not a project. Treat it with honour.
"Do you not know that your bodies are temples of the Holy Spirit...?" (1 Corinthians 6:19–20, NIV)

Order:
Set rhythms for rest, hydration, movement and nourishment.

Discipline:
Commit to persistence over convenience.

Example:
You plan meals that give life, protect your sleep and commit to moving your body, not for perfection, but for stewardship.

---

4. Family: Governing Your Atmosphere

Priority:
Value your family as a gift and responsibility.

"Honour your father and your mother..." (Exodus 20:12, NIV)

Chapter 4: Management - Bringing Order from Chaos

Order:
Create space for healthy relationships. Clarify boundaries that protect peace.

Discipline:
Again, choose persistence over convenience, especially in love, patience and communication.

Example:
You initiate open, respectful conversations with your parents, even when it's uncomfortable, because honour grows through humility. You schedule undistracted time with your spouse or children. You create margin for your home to be a sanctuary.

---

5. Community: Governing Your Connections

Priority:
Not every relationship is equal. Invest where there is alignment and life.
"Bad company corrupts good character." (1 Corinthians 15:33, NIV)

Order:
Define who belongs in your inner circle. Make room for mutual sharpening.

Discipline:
Release relationships that drain you spiritually. Protect your emotional availability.

Example:
You intentionally reach out to friends who build you up in faith. You check your motives before entering conversations, *"Am I here to serve or to be seen?"*

---

6. Work: Governing Your Assignment

Priority:
Work is not your identity, it's an assignment.
"Commit to the Lord whatever you do and He will establish your plans." (Proverbs 16:3, NIV)

Order:
Create structure for productivity: priorities, breaks and boundaries.

Discipline:
Do the small, consistent tasks even when they feel mundane.

***Example**:*
You plan your week in advance. You pace your workflow with rest.
You refuse to confuse busyness with fruitfulness.

---

7. Wealth: Governing Your Resources and Relationships

Priority:
Wealth includes more than money, it includes time, skills, relationships and opportunities.
"Moreover, it is required in stewards that one be found faithful." (1 Corinthians 4:2, NIV)

Order:
Budget your finances, track your giving and steward your connections with wisdom.

Discipline:
Avoid impulse. Plan with purpose. Practice generosity.

***Example**:*
You tithe faithfully, invest in your development and choose to

be generous with your time and counsel, knowing every resource is a seed.

The Flow of Divine Management of Who You Are

"The Kingdom of God is righteousness, peace and joy in the Holy Spirit." (Romans 14:17, NIV)

Righteousness sets your priorities.
Peace flows from order.
Joy rises through disciplined living.

You don't earn righteousness,
You receive it by being in Christ.
It is your position, not your performance.
And from that place of grace, peace flows,
Through trust, surrender, and acceptance.
Joy then follows, not from striving,
But from living in the security of peace
And the hope found in God's Word.

This is management in the Kingdom:
Not chaos, but clarity.
Not burden, but balance.
Not performance, but presence.

Let's now gather all this wisdom,
And anchor it in one final rhythm,
A cadence that invites peace,
And prepares you for what comes next.

Closing Thoughts

In this chapter, we learned that **management is the bridge between movement and maturity**.

This Is Love, Not Religion

It is not about control, it's about bringing **alignment and structure** to what God has already entrusted.

We studied the **Spirit of Understanding**,
Who teaches us not just what is true, but **how to live it out** wisely.
Understanding gives revelation its framework.
It leads to clarity, righteous action and spiritual maturity.

We explored **Day Four of creation**, where God placed the sun, moon and stars into the heavens.
Not just to shine, but to **govern**.
He didn't create more matter, He gave movement its meaning through time, order and rhythm.

Through the example of Moses and Jethro, we saw that even divine leadership can fail without systems.
Moses didn't need to do more, he needed to **delegate, organise and align**.

I shared my own journey into management, how God used wisdom, provision and obedience, to teach me that **order invites peace** and **faithfulness multiplies fruit**.

You are not just called to move things, you are called to guard what is holy while you do.

True management begins with worship: To serve with your hands and protect with your heart.

We then applied the **P.O.D. System**: Priority, Order, Discipline, across the seven areas of life: Godliness, Mindset, Well-being, Family, Community, Work and Wealth.
Each domain revealed the power of boundaries, clarity and Spirit-led stewardship.

Righteousness anchors your priorities. Peace flows from order. Joy flows through discipline.

Chapter 4: Management - Bringing Order from Chaos

This is divine management: A life arranged in heaven's rhythm, not earth's rush.

Management is not a burden,
It's how we build with wisdom.

It protects what's sacred.
It multiplies what's entrusted.
It carries what vision alone cannot sustain.

It's the practice of peace.
The blueprint for fruitfulness.
The rhythm of heaven written into your daily life.

Because without order, even brilliance burns out.
But with rhythm, even ordinary moments become eternal offerings.

So tend what God gave you.
Steward what He's already spoken.
And let your life become a sanctuary of strategy and rest.

Because once the structure is set,
God fills it with beauty.

Next, we move into **Artistry**,
Where insight becomes impact,
And creativity flows from presence,
Not performance.

Let's discover how wisdom becomes visible
Through the work of your hands.

Prayer Decreeing Management: Bringing My Life into Order

I am not called to chaos,
I am called to live with wisdom, rhythm and peace.

God is not the author of confusion,
But of clarity, structure and divine timing *(1 Corinthians 14:33)*.
I am filled with the Spirit of Understanding *(Isaiah 11:2)*,
Who teaches me not just what to do,
But how to walk in it.

I do not waste what God has given me.
I manage it with excellence.
I set priorities in line with His will (Matthew 6:33).
I bring order to my world through the Word (Psalm 119:105).
I discipline my actions so they reflect heaven's purpose (1 Corinthians 9:27).

My time is not random, it is appointed (Ecclesiastes 3:1).
My energy is not scattered, it is stewarded (1 Peter 4:10).
My gifts are not chaotic, they are aligned (Romans 12:6).

In every area of my life: godliness, mindset, well-being, family, community, work and wealth,
I walk in wisdom, clarity and intentional grace.

I do not chase more.
I steward what's already in my hands.

I live at the pace of heaven.
I build what lasts.
I govern what grows.
I honour what flows.

In Jesus' name.
Amen.

Chapter 4: Management - Bringing Order from Chaos

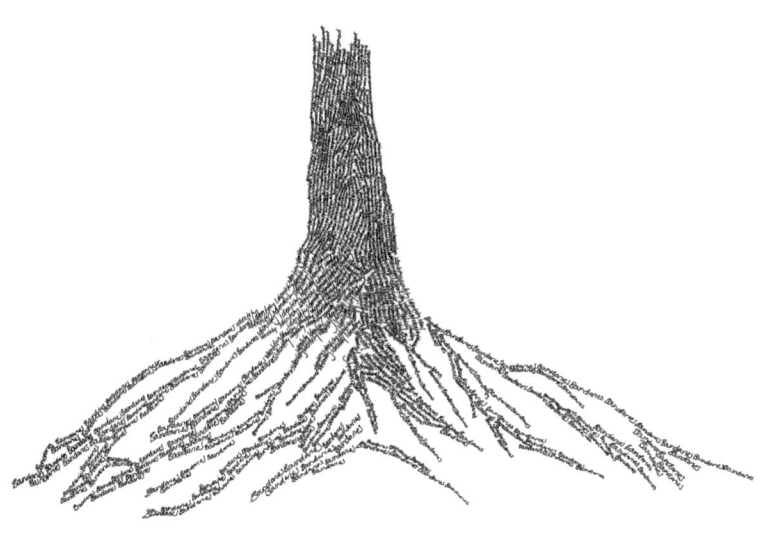

Chapter 5: Artistry - Creating from the Inside Out

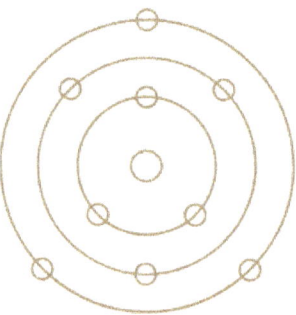

"And God said, Let the waters bring forth abundantly the moving creature that hath life, and fowl that may fly above the earth in the open firmament of heaven. And God created great whales, and every living creature that moveth, which the waters brought forth abundantly, after their kind, and every winged fowl after his kind: and God saw that it was good. And God blessed them, saying, Be fruitful, and multiply, and fill the waters in the seas, and let fowl multiply in the earth. And the evening and the morning were the fifth day."
(Genesis 1:20–23, KJV)

What Is Artistry?

Artistry is more than being creative,
It is the clear and intentional expression of truth.

Chapter 5: Artistry - Creating from the Inside Out

Not just what looks good,
But what reveals what is real.
What's meaningful.
What's rooted in wisdom.

Artistry is what happens when:
Insight finds structure.
Revelation meets rhythm.
Spirit and skill work together.

It's not performance,
It's presence.
Not just talent,
It's truth in motion.
Not just creativity,
It's clarity with purpose.

Artistry is how heaven's order and beauty show up in your hands.

Artistry is a creative skill, but not a chaotic one.
Each part is uniquely gifted, yet comes together in harmony.
Like stars stretched across the universe, seas teeming with life,
Or the air above, moving in ordered flow.

Or consider the human body:
Muscles, organs, breath, and bone,
Each distinct, yet made to move together.
What seems separate is actually synchronised.

This is creativity in its highest form:
A system, not just a spark.
A living structure, not just scattered brilliance.
Artistry reveals beauty not only in the detail,
But in the divine design where all parts sing together.

It doesn't just move emotions,
It multiplies meaning.
It teaches.

It reflects.
It transforms.

Like bees in a hive,
Each one designed with delicate precision,
Dancing, building, pollinating...
Artistry works both in the detail and in the design.
Each act has its own grace,
But it's part of a larger harmony that sustains life.

Like planets in orbit,
Each one spinning, shifting, glowing,
Together they create balance, rhythm, and awe.
The beauty of artistry is not just in what each part is,
But in how everything works together to reveal something far greater.

When you walk in artistry,
You're not just making something beautiful,
You're letting something eternal be seen.
You become part of the masterpiece.
A living brushstroke in the painting of divine purpose.

The Rooted Spirit Manifested: The Spirit of Wisdom

The *Spirit of Wisdom* doesn't just give you information,
It teaches you how to build with it.

This is the *mind of God in motion*,
Turning insight into something you can see, touch, and live.

Wisdom takes knowledge and understanding
And shapes them into fruit,
Something real, useful, and lasting.

Chapter 5: Artistry - Creating from the Inside Out

Where the Spirit of Understanding helps you *manage* what you've been given,
The Spirit of Wisdom helps you *build* what truly matters.

It's not just about knowing what's right,
It's about doing it well.

That's where true artistry begins:

It's the fingerprint of divine wisdom moving through you,
Where insight becomes impact.
Where clarity becomes expression.
Where obedience becomes legacy.

Wisdom says:

*"You don't just carry revelation,
You carry design.
And when you build with Me,
Heaven echoes through your work."*

When the Spirit of Wisdom flows through you,
Your creativity becomes a mirror, reflecting God's brilliance.

Not through perfection,
But through practiced, purposeful excellence.

Wisdom is more than intelligence,
It is the lifeline that flows through all things,
So that the glory of God can be recognised.

Everything must flow.

Where flow is honoured, life flourishes.
Where flow is blocked, something begins to die.

Look at the body:
When blood clots in the wrong place, life is in danger.
The restriction becomes a warning.
The system breaks down.

This Is Love, Not Religion

The same is true in the soul.

When someone gives but cannot receive,
They slowly wither under the weight of imbalance.
When someone tries to control what God asked them to steward,
What was once alive becomes stagnant.
Overprotection turns into limitation.
Flow becomes fear.

Wisdom teaches rhythm.
It teaches us how to move with God's design.
To honour both action and rest.
To give and receive.
To plant and release.

This is why we are not called to dominate,
But to manage with reverence.

To steward all things in respect to God's glory,
Which is revealed through the virtues He embodies:
Love. Patience. Kindness. Faithfulness. And more.

When wisdom flows, so does life.
And where there is life, God is glorified.

Creation and the Fifth Day

Before there was form, there was water.

In Hebrew, the word for water, *mayim* (מַיִם), has no singular form.
It is plural by nature, like wisdom, flowing in many directions at once.

From Day One, when the Spirit hovered over the deep,
To Day Two, when God separated the waters above from

Chapter 5: Artistry - Creating from the Inside Out

below,
Water has always carried divine potential.

It is alive.
Dynamic.
Essential.

In *mayim*, we see more than an element,
We see a system.
A life-giving, life-sustaining stream.
God's wisdom in motion.

And now, on Day Five, that wisdom begins to take shape.

Heavenly insight takes on tangible form.
Heavenly insight continues its earthly manifestation.
A sacred system, life-bearing and beautifully designed: artistry in motion.

The waters become a womb.
Life is drawn out, creatures of the sea, birds of the sky,
All bursting forth from the same source.

What was once still is now swimming and soaring.

God filled the sea and sky with movement, colour, and sound.
It was vibrant. Alive. Overflowing.

But it wasn't chaotic.
It was choreographed.

From the **depths**, He called forth movement.
Into the **sky**, He released song.

Each creature was made
According to its **kind**,
Not as replicas,
But as reflections of divine design.
And in their design, they multiplied.
Abundance wasn't manufactured.

This Is Love, Not Religion

It was the result of alignment.

This is artistry in motion.
Where divine depth meets creative expression,
Where purpose overflows through patterned life.
But let's take it a bristle further,
For even in wild side of creation,
There was order:
"Each according to their kind."
The first signs of life reflecting God appear in His command:
"Be fruitful."

To be fruitful means to be seeded.
To carry the genesis of something sacred,
Something that begins with the Creator Himself.

The creatures born on this day were the first to reflect God's intention:
To multiply what they had been entrusted with.

This is wisdom in motion.
The sacred system of boundary, identity, animation, and management,
All leading to *artistry*.

A cycle that carries the divine pattern:

Seed → Fruit → Seed again.

Even birds and fish,
Both drawn from the waters,
Often emerge first as eggs.

Hidden, encased, but filled with potential.
Just like us.
Born first by flesh,
from the waters of our mothers womb,
Brought to this world
Then called out of darkness by Christ alone
To be reborn by Spirit (through baptism)

Chapter 5: Artistry - Creating from the Inside Out

To fully live in our divine domain.

This is artistry refined by transformation,
Matured by rhythm,
And empowered by design.

Even creativity had structure.

Then God gave a clear command:

"Be fruitful. Multiply. Fill the earth."

This was more than a call to reproduce.
It was a call to carry meaning forward,
To leave a legacy.

But not all who understand God's patterns seek to honour them.
There are forces,
Subtle, cruel, and convincing,
That twist divine design for destruction.

Demonic powers do not ignore God's wisdom.
They manipulate it.
They draw from the waters of wisdom,
But poison the stream.

What God meant to give life,
They use to bring death.

Scripture makes it plain:
"The thief comes only to steal, kill, and destroy." (John 10:10, NIV)

This is the counterfeit wisdom,
Not from above, but born of envy, pride, and rebellion.
It breaks the rhythm of creation.
It interrupts fruitfulness with barrenness.
It names death as freedom,
And calls rebellion truth.

This is the wisdom of the world,
That seduces us to believe:
"What is bad is good," (Isaiah 5:20)
"What is good is outdated," (Proverbs 22:28)
And even *"What is holy is restrictive."*

But the true wisdom of God
Always produces life,
In alignment, in clarity, in peace.
That's what artistry does.

It's not just self-expression, it's legacy-building.
It's how our creative work outlives us.

True artistry doesn't just shine in a moment.
It creates momentum.
It multiplies impact.

It reflects God's divine rhythm: Alive.
Ordered.
Purposeful.

When you align with that rhythm,
You don't just create,
You *co-create*.

A Living Example: Moses the Visionary Builder *(Exodus 25–31)*

Moses wasn't just a leader.
He was a *receiver*.

On Mount Sinai, God gave him detailed instructions for building the Tabernacle,
Every material. Every colour. Every measurement.

Chapter 5: Artistry - Creating from the Inside Out

It wasn't about decoration.
It was about *divine design*.

God said,

"Make everything according to the pattern I showed you."
(*Exodus 25:40, NIV*)

Moses didn't build from imagination,
He built from *revelation*.

And he didn't build alone.

God filled Bezalel with the Spirit,
Skilled in every kind of craft,
So the vision could be brought to life with *excellence*.

This is the flow of godly artistry:

- Revelation comes before construction.
- Worship comes before workmanship.
- Presence comes before productivity.

Moses translated what he saw in God's presence
Into something visible, usable, and holy.

That's what creative obedience looks like.

You may not be building a Tabernacle.
But if God gives you a pattern,
Your role is to carry it with *honour*.

Artistry is about stewarding what's sacred.
Turning divine insight into real-world impact.

The Scenario: When Creativity Lacks Flow

You know you carry something meaningful inside.
Not just ideas, but insight.
Not just talent, but purpose.

You've felt it when you create, when you speak, write, design, or dream.
But sometimes... it doesn't connect.

You're creating, but it feels stuck.
It looks good, but it doesn't go deep.
It's moving, but it's not multiplying.

That's the tension of unrooted artistry.

You want your work to carry power, not just polish.
You want it to reflect truth, not just talent.

You're not looking for applause.
You're looking for impact.

That longing?
It's the Spirit of Wisdom calling you to create with clarity and purpose.

When creativity connects with divine understanding,
Art doesn't just express, it transforms.

My Turning Point: Learning to Create with Wisdom

1. The Ache of Awareness

Life often calls us to figure things out
To chase, strive, and survive within systems we don't even like.

Chapter 5: Artistry - Creating from the Inside Out

Let's be honest: this world is deeply broken.

In my early walk with Christ, one of the first things my heart grieved over
was the corruption in the health industry.

At the root? The love of money.
What I felt wasn't just frustration
It was a holy anger.
A divine ache over how things have been set up to keep us blind.

So blind that when the truth appears, we think it's a lie.

---

2. The Twisted Reflection

It's the same with Christ.
He is so true that the world sees Him as false.
And honestly, when even believers struggle to hold firm,
Who can blame the world for doubting?

But God began to show me something deeper:
The systems of this world are twisted reflections
Of what He originally called good.

And one day, He will establish His Kingdom once and for all,
A vision of wisdom too vast for the mind to comprehend.

---

3. The Artist's Awakening

I was captivated by the details of how things are.
I almost missed what God was trying to show me:
Artistry, how His wisdom is the root of a life that bears fruit.

Everything that exists is different,

Separate,
Yet one.

Like the Trinity:
Distinct in function,
Yet unified in meaning, vision, and purpose.
And like us.

---

4. Formed to Fit

I began to realise:
I have a role in this divine design.
Me, flawed, but intentionally formed.

My uniqueness wasn't an accident.
It was a deliberate contribution to God's wisdom.

But understanding that took time.

God patiently ordered my steps,
Revealing one slice of truth at a time,
Never more than I could carry.

---

5. The Detour of Hustle

And yes, my steps wandered.
I chased side hustles and get-rich schemes,
Even while heading towards nearly £20,000 of debt.
I thought I needed to find the perfect system.
But there was too much information.
Too many distractions.
Too many reasons to feel entitled.

And then, God.

6. The Eden Pattern

He showed me that He had been shaping my life the same way He shaped Adam's:

God formed Adam
Adam didn't design himself.

God prepared Eden
And only then placed Adam in it.

God gave Adam commands
Not to control, but to instruct and sustain life.

God brought Eve to Adam
Not through striving, but through staying in position.

---

7. Christ, the Mirror

We see this same pattern in the life of Jesus:
Formed in the secret place,
Walking in obedience,
Fulfilling every command,
And awaiting full union with His bride, the Church.

God had been forming me too.
In hiddenness.
In service.
In the unseen.

---

8. The Naming of Ailey

He prepared spaces for me, first in retail,

Then as a basketball player and coach,
While shaping me as a coach for lives.

And He even gave me a name:
Ailey.

I had been praying for a new business name.
"Life Maestro" was my first idea,
But it felt self-centred.

Then, in prayer, a new word unfolded.

First came *"Ley"*
A piece of land used temporarily for rest and pasture,
Often rotated with crops.

Then, whilst continuing in prayer,
"Ai" came in front, completing the name: Ailey

Ailey, meaning light.

---

9. A Prophetic Identity

As I reflected, I realised it wasn't random.
It was prophetic.

I saw myself as one who tends God's land,
Preparing the ground,
Sowing truth,
And trusting that in this pasture of growth,
His light would bring wisdom, healing, and peace.

This framework, the one you're reading now,
Was forged through perseverance.

Chapter 5: Artistry - Creating from the Inside Out

10. The Word that Carried Me

A perseverance rooted in a word God spoke to me
During one of my lowest seasons:

"Be patient."
And He meant it.

Through every setback,
Every challenge,
And every breakthrough,
God was refining me into a vessel of His wisdom.

---

11. A Framework Becomes a Testimony

The moment I saw it all coming together?
I was on the phone with a friend.

We were talking about life, our challenges, our prayers,
And suddenly, God's presence descended.

It was as Scripture says:

"For where two or three gather in my name, there am I with them."
(Matthew 18:20, NIV)

In that moment,
I stumbled through a raw, unrehearsed version of each step,
From boundaries to love.

And I knew:
This wasn't just a process.

It was a testimony.

A framework that gives glory to God.

A rhythm designed to help us live well.

---

12. The Glory and the Groaning

In the years that followed,
God deepened that understanding.

Some days, I'd dance in my apartment,
Rejoicing over revelation.

Other days, I'd be in Costa,
Frozen by the weight of what He had just revealed.

Sometimes I'd just smile quietly,
Holding my composure,
While inwardly in awe of the insight He'd entrusted to me.

Not every season felt glorious.
There were times I wondered if He had left me.
But He hadn't.
He was always there.

---

13. The God Who Tests to Entrust

In the silence, He was testing my heart,
Not to punish me,
But to see where I would lean...
And to prepare me for what was coming.

He gave me only what I could carry at each stage.

And with time,
I trusted I could live it,
And then share it.

Chapter 5: Artistry - Creating from the Inside Out

14. The Thumbprint Vision

I remember thinking:
God, how much of You is this?
You're showing me who You are in a way I've never seen before.

And then I saw a vision:

A starry sky stretched above me.
From the right came a massive thumb.

It appeared in the sky and filled the heavens.

Within the thumbprint,
One line was highlighted.

Just a tiny fragment.
Seemingly insignificant.

But it was God's thumb.
He humbled my thoughts on how big the framework is compared to Him.

15. Entrusted, Not Authored

This framework? These chapters?
They were never authored by me.

They were entrusted to me.

They are meant to serve.
To reflect.
To play their part in God's greater wisdom.

16. Still Learning, Still Creating

And God continues to guide me,
Because I continue to ask for wisdom.
For the fullness of the Holy Spirit.

And for that to happen,
I must decrease.

Just as Christ did:

"The Spirit of the Lord shall rest upon Him…"
(Isaiah 11:2, NIV)

"he made himself nothing…"
(Philippians 2:7–8, NIV)

"And the Spirit of God descended like a dove…"
(Matthew 3:16, NIV)

So here I am,
Still learning.
Still repenting.
Still surrendering.

And still creating…
From the inside out.

Practicing Artistry in Daily Life: The S.O.W. Rhythm

Artistry doesn't begin with ambition.
It begins with *attention*.

Chapter 5: Artistry - Creating from the Inside Out

It begins when you pause, listen and move with God, not ahead of Him.

The work of creation is sacred.
And sacred things grow in rhythm, not rush.

That's why I no longer chase output, I follow the flow.
I live by this rhythm: **S.O.W.**
Seek. Obey. Witness.

Because what you create isn't just about you.
It's about what heaven wants to reveal *through* you.

Seek: Start With Prayer and Insight

"If any of you lacks wisdom, let him ask of God..." (James 1:5, NIV)

Everything meaningful begins in stillness.
Before God created man, He formed the ground. Before Jesus ministered, He withdrew to pray.
Before you build, *seek*.

Ask the questions:

- *"What are You revealing, Lord?"*
- *"What's the burden You've placed in me?"*
- *"What do You want me to carry in this season?"*

Seeking is not hesitation, it's honour.
You honour the process by starting in His presence.

Real-life example:
You receive a phrase, a vision, or a desire to help someone. You don't run with it immediately, you sit with it.
You pray, reflect, journal. You ask God what He wants to do with what He's placed in your heart.
And when you seek with humility, clarity begins to form.

Obey: Build With What's in Your Hand

"Whatever He says to you, do it." (John 2:5, NIV)
"Whoever hears these words of mine and puts them into practice..." (Matthew 7:24, NIV)

Insight without action is inspiration wasted.
Obedience is what turns revelation into legacy.

This doesn't mean you have to have it all figured out.
It means you trust God enough to move when He says move.
You don't need a full plan, you just need a step.

Real-life example:
You don't wait for a platform, you write the first sentence.
You take what's in your hand, your sketchpad, your voice, your phone, your idea, and you begin.
It's messy at first. But movement activates refinement.

You obey and through obedience, the work begins to breathe.

Witness: Watch the Work Mature and Multiply

"And the earth brought forth..." (Genesis 1:12, NIV)
"You will recognise them by their fruit." (Matthew 7:16, NIV)

When you sow in faith, you begin to see fruit.
Not always fast, not always flashy, but always faithful.

Witnessing is the part you don't control.
It's when others begin to see what God has been forming in you.

Chapter 5: Artistry - Creating from the Inside Out

And more importantly, it's when *you* begin to see that what once lived only in prayer... now lives in public space.

Real-life example:
What started as a whisper in your spirit becomes a word for someone else.
A blog post turns into a conversation.
A song heals a wound.
A class you taught unlocks identity.
The art you made in tears becomes someone else's turning point.

Your work speaks, not to impress, but to *express* what heaven planted in you.

The Creative Rhythm of S.O.W.

Seek: Listen before you move
Obey: Walk with what you've been given
Witness: Let God bring the increase

This is not a hustle.
This is not performance.
This is **Spirit-led artistry**.
And like the animation journey, grass, herb, and tree,
You grow in expression as you remain faithful to what God has placed in you.

So pause.
Seek Him.
Obey what He shows.
And witness what He grows.

Because when your creativity flows in His rhythm,
You don't just make things...
You *multiply meaning*.

Closing Thoughts

In this chapter, we explored **artistry as the visible expression of divine wisdom**, not just creative output, but Spirit-filled obedience in form.

We encountered the **Spirit of Wisdom**, who enables us to not only receive insight, but build with it.
Where understanding manages what is given, wisdom **shapes it into impact**.

We looked at **Day Five of creation**, where God filled the waters and the skies with movement, sound and life.
It wasn't random, it was rhythmic. Each creature was made *"according to its kind,"* showing us that **creativity has structure, legacy and intent**.

Moses became our example, not just as a deliverer, but as a **visionary builder**.
He received a divine pattern and stewarded it into something tangible, holy and lasting.

I shared my turning point. Not performance, but revelation. Where I stopped chasing and started receiving.

Where creativity became less about me and more about Him. Not for applause. But alignment. Not to impress. But to agree. To create, not for the world but as a witness to God.

And through the **S.O.W. rhythm, Seek, Obey, Witness**, we saw how Spirit-led creativity moves:
We seek God first.
We obey with what's in our hand.
We witness as the fruit multiplies in His time.

Artistry is not about perfection.
It's about **presence, precision and partnership with God**.

Chapter 5: Artistry - Creating from the Inside Out

Artistry isn't noise, it's nuance.
It isn't trend, it's truth in motion.

You weren't made to create for approval.
You were made to create from alignment.

Let what's within you rise.
Let wisdom guide your hands.
Let heaven speak through your expression.

You don't need a spotlight.
You need surrender.

Because when you create from the inside out,
Your work becomes more than art,
It becomes a **mirror of glory**,
A living echo of God's design.

But even creativity must walk in clarity.
Expression without direction is movement without meaning.

Next, we step into **Purpose**.
Where what flows through your hands
Finds its alignment with what lives in your core.

Prayer Decreeing Artistry: Creating with Purpose

I am not just creative, I am divinely designed to reflect the wisdom of God.

I am filled with the Spirit of Wisdom *(Exodus 31:3)*,
Equipped for every good work *(2 Timothy 3:17)*,
And called to create with excellence, not for applause, but for impact.

I carry insight and revelation,
And I release it with order and clarity.

This Is Love, Not Religion

My work is not random,
It is a reflection of heaven's design.

I am a co-creator with God *(1 Corinthians 3:9)*.
I don't chase perfection, I steward purpose.
My gift multiplies when rooted in obedience.
My creativity is not just for expression, it's for transformation.

I build what God shows me.
Like Moses, I follow the pattern *(Exodus 25:40)*.
Like Bezalel, I am filled with skill, understanding and divine ability *(Exodus 31:3–5)*.

I release what's in my hand.
I speak what God has placed in my spirit.
I create with boldness, discipline and grace.

I am not just making art,
I am building legacy.
And everything I create carries heaven's fingerprint.

In Jesus' name.
Amen.

Chapter 5: Artistry - Creating from the Inside Out

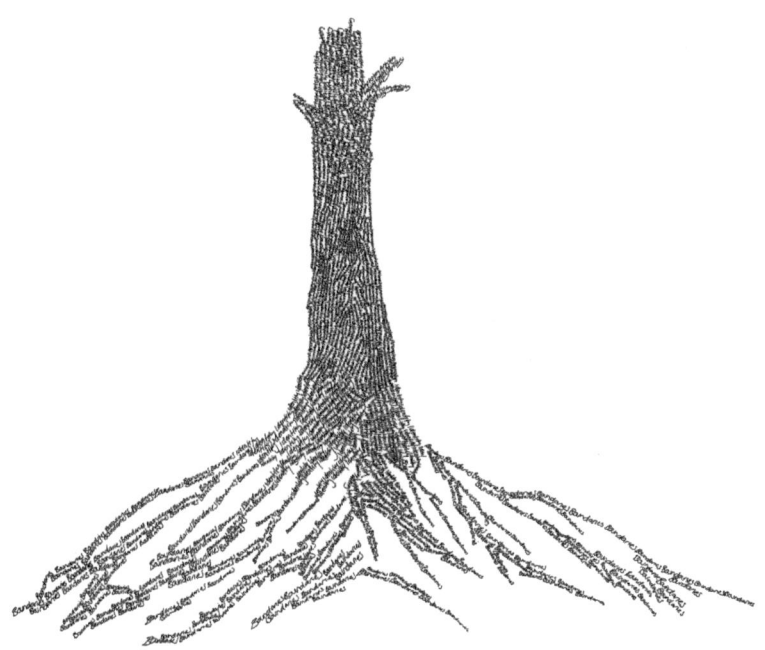

Chapter 6: Purpose - Walking in Your Divine Design

"And God said, Let the earth bring forth the living creature after his kind... And God said, Let us make man in our image, after our likeness: and let them have dominion... And God blessed them, and God said unto them, Be fruitful, and multiply, and replenish the earth, and subdue it: and have dominion... And God saw every thing that He had made, and, behold, it was very good. And the evening and the morning were the sixth day." (Genesis 1:24–31, KJV)

What Is Purpose?

Purpose is not performance.
It's *partnership*.

It's not striving to earn,
It's stewarding what's already been entrusted.

Chapter 6: Purpose - Walking in Your Divine Design

Purpose is where your identity finds assignment.
Where your gifts meet grace.
Where your life becomes a mirror of God's glory.

In the beginning, God didn't just form humanity, He *commissioned* them:

"Be fruitful. Multiply. Replenish. Subdue. Have dominion." (Genesis 1:28, NIV)

This is more than a mandate.
It's a *divine design*.

- **Image**: Who you are in God
- **Likeness**: How you reflect Him
- **Fruitfulness**: Character that reproduces
- **Multiplication**: Impact that expands
- **Replenishing**: Restoration through your presence
- **Subduing**: Authority over chaos
- **Dominion**: Leadership that looks like love

Purpose isn't about doing more.
It's about *becoming* who you were always meant to be.

But purpose without purity becomes pressure.
And not all purpose is divine, so discern the source.

The enemy offers shortcuts:

- Success without surrender
- Applause without alignment
- Fruit with no seed

It looks good.
Feels good.
But it's hollow.
Temporary.

The Kingdom moves differently:

- Purpose rooted in process
- Fruit that grows through seedtime and harvest

It's slower, but *eternal*.

So be discerning.
Not every open door is divine.
Not every platform is pure.

Some "success" is built on:

- Manipulation
- Pride
- Control
- Comparison
- Compromise
- Hidden agendas

But true Kingdom fruit grows from:

- Integrity
- Humility
- Stewardship
- Patience
- Faith
- Love
- Joy in the process

Because purpose without purity will always rot.
But purpose rooted in God's power,
Will always *remain*.

The Difference Between Purpose and Calling

Your purpose is your reason for being.
Your calling is how that purpose is expressed in a particular season.

Chapter 6: Purpose - Walking in Your Divine Design

Purpose is the seed.
Calling is the fruit.

Purpose is eternal.
Calling is seasonal.

Purpose never changes.
Callings evolve with time, growth and obedience.

When we confuse the two, we chase platforms instead of presence.
We measure impact by visibility instead of faithfulness.

But when you understand that your purpose is to reflect God,
To reveal His nature through your design,
You stop waiting for a stage.
You start stewarding the soil.

Even when your life nears its end,
The fruit you leave behind carries seeds,
Seeds that rest in the soil for a new spring.

Because Kingdom purpose doesn't die with us.
It multiplies beyond us.

Purpose is not just something you discover,
It's something you're born with.

It is a seed, planted by God before you ever took your first breath.
It is your reason, woven into your design, shaping how you see the world and how you serve in it.
And it is your driver, the Spirit-led pull that compels you to move, act and create in alignment with heaven.

Seed. Reason. Driver.
Planted in eternity. Revealed in time. Activated by faith.

And because God disperses seeds according to need, not just your plans,
Don't limit how He may use your harvest.

Just be faithful with the fruit...
And trust Him with where the next seed will grow.

The Rooted Spirit Manifested: The Spirit of Might

The *Spirit of Might* is divine power in motion.
It doesn't just strengthen you,
It sustains you.

This is the supernatural force that carries you beyond your limits,
So you can fulfil God's will with courage and conviction.

It is the Spirit that empowers action,
Not for striving,
But for sacred assignments.

It breathes strength into your bones
When your calling feels too heavy,
Too costly,
Too hard.

Purpose may begin with calling,
But it matures through *might*.

The Spirit of Might brings clarity to your "why"
And endurance to your "how."

It enables you to stand.
To move.
To build.
To finish.

Chapter 6: Purpose - Walking in Your Divine Design

It whispers:

*"You are stronger than you feel,
Because you were made for more than you know."*

The Spirit of Might equips you to walk through resistance with resolve,
Not by your strength,
But by *His*.

And in doing so,
It moves you from potential...
To purpose.

Creation and the Sixth Day

*"Then God said, 'Let the land produce living creatures according to their kinds...'
God made the wild animals according to their kinds, the livestock according to their kinds...
Then God said, 'Let us make mankind in our image, in our likeness, so that they may rule...'"*
(Genesis 1:24–31, KJV)

When your life feels formless, you've lost sight of your **image**.
When it feels void, you're disconnected from your **likeness**.

"Formless" isn't just confusion,
It's drifting away from who you are.
"Void" isn't just emptiness,
It's the absence of purposeful expression.

That's why the sixth day matters.

Because in the image of God, you are called to embody *form*, clarity, intention, and identity.
And in the likeness of God, you are designed to move with *function*, action, expression, and purpose.

This Is Love, Not Religion

When both come together, you don't just exist,
You become a living reflection of divine design.

And this doesn't just apply to who you are,
It applies to everything you do.

Every action needs intention.
Every task needs alignment.

Because when purpose is absent, even good things become formless.
And when intention is ignored, emptiness takes root.

A life without purpose becomes a land where anarchy and chaos can grow,
Not because of evil, but because of *aimlessness*.

Just as in creation, God didn't leave the earth formless and void.
He filled it with meaning.
And He calls you to do the same with your thoughts, relationships and life.

Day Six marks not just the forming of life, but the *entrusting* of it.

Humanity was not just made to function, but to govern, multiply and reflect.
Purpose is God's imprint moving through your life.

God filled the land with life,
Creatures of every kind,
Moving in their element,
Each made to function by design.

Then, God said something different:
"Let us make man in our image."

Humanity was not a replication.
It was a *reflection*.

Chapter 6: Purpose - Walking in Your Divine Design

Not just of God's creativity,
But of His *authority*.

To humanity, He gave dominion, not to exploit, but to steward.
Over land. Over animals. Over resources.
Dominion means responsibility, not control.
A call to cultivate, not consume...

He didn't just give us breath.
He gave us *blessing*.

"Be fruitful. Multiply. Subdue. Replenish."

This was not just instruction.
It was *identity*.

The animals had instinct.
But man was given *insight*.

We were formed to reflect,
And filled to fulfil.

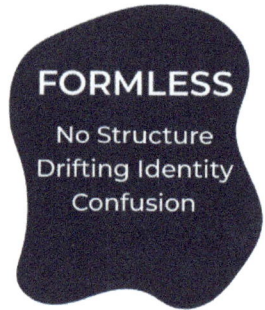

FORMLESS

No Structure
Drifting Identity
Confusion

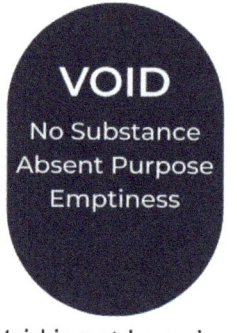

VOID

No Substance
Absent Purpose
Emptiness

Formless is not knowing who you are

Void is not knowing why you are here

"Then God said, 'Let us make mankind in our image, in our likeness, so that they may rule…'"
(Genesis 1:26, KJV)

IMAGE
(Who you are)

Identity
Form
Clarity
Intention

LIKENESS
(How you move)

Purpose
Function
Expression
Action

When Image and Likeness come together, you don't just exist, you embody divine design.

Chapter 6: Purpose - Walking in Your Divine Design

A Living Example: Moses at the Red Sea (Exodus 14)

Moses wasn't just called to free Israel,
He was called to *lead* them into freedom.

But when they reached the Red Sea,
He faced the impossible:

- A blocked path
- A panicking people
- An approaching army

And in that moment, God didn't give him a plan,
He gave him a *posture*.

"The Lord will fight for you; you need only to be still."
(Exodus 14:14, NIV)

And then:

"Raise your staff... divide the waters."
(Exodus 14:16, NIV)

God had positioned Moses not to *react*,
But to *respond*.

The staff in his hand wasn't just a tool.
It was a *testimony*,
A reminder of God's power working through surrender.
What made him look weak and humble was the very space
God chose to reveal His strength.

So he lifted it. And the sea parted.

The sea responded to *alignment*, not effort.
And the impossible bowed to *authority*.

This was the Spirit of Might in motion.
Not human strength,
But divine empowerment.

Purpose didn't look like a plan.
It looked like *trust*.

And that's what the Spirit of Might does:

- It empowers you to stand when fear says run.
- To move when logic says wait.
- To obey when the outcome is still unseen.

Because the One who calls you forward,
The same One who said,

"Why are you crying to Me? Tell the people to move forward."
(*Exodus 14:15, NIV*)

Will part the sea
When you lift your hand.

Your purpose is like that. You don't have to create it,
You have to *cultivate* it.

It's already in your hands.
It's already in your design.

The Scenario: The Vision with No Fuel

There is a moment in every heart when hunger rises,
A desire to live for something more.
More than surviving.
More than striving.

You sense that your life was designed with meaning,

Chapter 6: Purpose - Walking in Your Divine Design

That you weren't just born, you were sent.
That there is something only you can carry.

But when passion meets uncertainty,
When calling feels distant,
And when waiting feels like wasting,
You begin to question the design.

You ask:
Am I called?
Am I late?
Am I enough?

This is the ache of misaligned purpose.
When you know there's more within you,
But haven't yet seen the path before you.

You've felt the pull.
You've glimpsed the vision.
But the next step is still unclear.

And that's when God begins to speak.
Not with a roadmap,
But with a mirror.

My Turning Point: The Yielded Trust

1. The Misunderstood Grind

I used to think purpose was a grind.
Something you earned.
Something you chased.

And though I believed in God,
I didn't yet understand what it meant to be *powered* by God.

This Is Love, Not Religion

I wanted to walk in purpose,
But I was walking in my own strength.
And every step felt heavy.

---

2. The Quiet Surrender

The shift came quietly... but completely.
I realised: my strength wasn't the source, His was.

I surrendered, not just the dream,
But the ability to achieve it.

And everything began to change.
I prayed differently.
Worked differently.
Expected differently.

And for the first time, I saw the difference between effort and anointing.

---

3. The Fire of a Vow

"Seek first the kingdom and His righteousness and all these things will be added unto you."
(Matthew 6:33, NIV)

That word came alive to me.

I remember it clearly, I was in Texas, burning with something I couldn't name.
A fire of purpose was rising... but I had no language for it.

I told myself: *I won't watch my favourite type of movies until this fire is fulfilled.*
(For context, I didn't even watch the first Black Panther or most of the latest Marvels until December 2024.)

Chapter 6: Purpose - Walking in Your Divine Design

The moment I made that vow in my heart,
I was given a vision.

---

4. A Glimpse of the Promise

I saw myself in the future:
Sitting on a couch, feet up, arms spread along the top,
Watching a small TV in a peaceful room.
I saw it from above.
Like my spirit was witnessing the promise before it arrived.

It wasn't the first time I'd seen that room.
In an earlier vision, I saw a space transform in front of my eyes,
The same space, but the kitchen was revealed.
I didn't understand it then.
But God was showing me something ahead of its time.

---

5. Carried in Homelessness

Years passed.
I was sofa-surfing.
Homeless, technically, bouncing between people's homes for seven months.
My job was in London,

but to make ends meet,

I had to let go of the place I had in Chelmsford.

Still, I carried peace.
I carried purpose.
Wherever I went, I chose to live truthfully,
Animating God's virtues.
Sharing what I could.
Being a vessel, even when I had nothing to my name.

6. A Witness in the Darkness

One friend, deep in depression, noticed something.
He stayed locked in his room, blinds drawn day and night.
But one day, he stepped out and said:

"I don't get it.
You're sleeping on my floor, but you're the one singing.
I'm in my room miserable… and you're out here with joy.
How come?"

I smiled.
"I already told you."

He knew what I meant.

He opened His heart to the Word,
And for the first time, he said:
"I think I'm starting to feel better about it."

7. The Fulfilled Vision

But that wasn't the end of the story.

During that seven month season,
I got a call from someone close.
They said:
"We want to give you a home."

I prayed.
I listened.
And through the Spirit, I picked the right one.

It wasn't until I moved in…
That I realised what had just happened.

Chapter 6: Purpose - Walking in Your Divine Design

I stood in the room,
And it hit me.
This was the room from the vision.
The couch. The layout. The kitchen. The stillness.

God had shown it to me before I ever arrived

---

8. The Remembered Promise

And now, I was living in what once felt impossible.

I remembered what He told me years ago:
"I will give you your life."

And through Abraham, Moses, David, Joseph, and yes, Jesus,
He showed me what that promise meant.

You see,
Purpose is not something we grind for.
It is something God builds in us.
And brings forth in His timing.

It doesn't start with ability.
It starts with alignment.

---

9. Divine Empowerment

The Spirit of Might is not brute strength.
It is divine empowerment,
That flows when your life is yielded.

---

10. Assignment by Alignment

In those seasons.

This Is Love, Not Religion

I found myself coaching basketball.
Not a path I pursued.
Not a dream I drafted.
But somehow, God placed me there.

It started in my first year back in London.
I signed to a semi-pro basketball team.
Part of the contract? Coaching.
From primary schools to university courts, I was placed where I never planned.

---

11. The Growth in Serving

Most days had me with children.
Teaching them the basics.
Showing them how to move, think and play.

And somehow, I knew, I was supposed to be there.
It wasn't glamorous.
It wasn't part of "the plan."
But it was full of God.

At first, I was just trying to earn.
But He was teaching me to serve.

Through coaching, patience grew.
Patience became understanding.
Understanding became care.
Care became love.
And love became intentional service.

---

12. The Formation of Virtue

I had always carried these virtues, somewhere.
But here, they were being forged.

Chapter 6: Purpose - Walking in Your Divine Design

The children adored me.
The teens respected me.
The teachers welcomed my presence.

I didn't just coach them to win, I coached them to think.
To reflect.
To become.
And in that process, something in me was becoming too.

---

13. The Birth of a Calling

My gifting with people began to sharpen.
Business instincts started to shape.
I saw how the core of every person, child or adult, longed to be seen, known, guided.

My interest in life coaching exploded.
I was drawn to it more, especially what I saw coming out of America.
The impact.
The transformation.
The freedom.
God let me see what was possible, through people, for people.

---

14. Favour in the Field

And He didn't stop there.

At the university level, I was still coaching,
And winning.

Every year, championships.
Men's teams.
Women's teams.
Seasons of favour.

Not by my brilliance.
But by His wisdom.
He gave me people.
He gave me insight.
He gave me victory.

---

15. A Framework From the Father

In life coaching, He gave me vision.
He revealed the framework that would change everything.
The structure.
The system.
The Spirit-breathed blueprint for transformation.

And it all started… because I honoured where I was.

---

16. Rooted and Raised

I tended the garden He placed me in.
And He grew me into the man I was becoming.

This is purpose.
Not chasing something out there,
But stewarding what's right here.

And from this place,
God built me.
Trained me.
Positioned me.

And though I still don't see it all,
I trust Him.

Because the One who plants us…
Is the One who grows us.

Chapter 6: Purpose - Walking in Your Divine Design

Practicing Purpose in Daily Life

Before purpose is practiced, it is perceived in the unseen.

The "Be–Do–Have" rhythm flows from invisible foundations:

- Be is character and identity, hidden roots in God.
- Do is alignment with His standards, quiet obedience.
- Have is fruit, the visible overflow of what was rooted in vision.

This isn't just a productivity model. It's a spiritual formation path.

Before you do great things, you become someone great in God.
Before you have impact, you carry integrity in silence.
From the beginning, God gave us a blueprint for purpose:

"Be fruitful and multiply and replenish the earth and subdue it: and have dominion."
(Genesis 1:28, NIV)

These aren't just commands.
They're a divine **sequence**, a **progression** for how purpose grows:

Be fruitful: Cultivate character and intimacy with God.
Multiply: Let what's in you overflow to others.
Replenish: Restore what's broken through presence and service.
Subdue: Bring order to what's chaotic.
Have dominion: Walk in authority rooted in love.

This is the pattern of divine purpose:
You **become**, then you **build** and from there, you **bless**.

You don't start with dominion, you grow into it.
And that growth begins right here, **in your daily practice**.

Stage 1: Be

Be: To be who you are called to be, you must have roots in the truth of whose you are.

Before you can walk in purpose, you must be who God created you to be. This means:

- Rooting yourself in truth.
- Understanding whose you are before figuring out what you do.
- Letting your identity take root in God's Word and His Spirit, not the shifting winds of circumstance.

Purpose flows from being. Your essence is your anchor (The Seven Spirits of God).

Stage 2: Do

Do: Growing in the Vine of truth gives you the confidence to do what you're supposed to do.

From the security of who you are, you are empowered to act. Doing is not about performance, it's about obedience to The Vine (The Seven Pillars).

- Move when prompted.
- Serve where placed.
- Grow where planted.

When you know who you are, you gain the courage to do what you've never done. Purpose isn't passive, it's participation.

Chapter 6: Purpose - Walking in Your Divine Design

Stage 3: Have

Have: When doing the things you're called to, the fruits you were made to steward will bloom.

When you are aligned in your being and faithful in your doing, you will have the fruit God designed for your life.

- Fruit in relationships.
- Fruit in influence.
- Fruit in legacy.

This is not about gain, it's about glory. The fruit is not yours to boast in. It's God's evidence in you. The fire evidence is Fruits of the Spirit and how they flourish in the Seven Areas of Life (Fruits of Life).

By becoming someone you've never been, you'll begin to do things in ways you've never done and then you will have what you've never had.

This is the divine rhythm of calling:

Root: The Spirit empowers your purpose
Vine: The structure of your life in Christ
Fruit: The visible impact across the seven areas of life

We don't chase results. We tend our roots.
We don't force outcomes. We remain in the Vine.
We don't self-power. We yield to the Spirit.
And God brings the increase.

You don't **start** with dominion, you **grow** into it. Let your daily practice reflect the divine pattern:

- **Be** rooted.
- **Do** in obedience.
- **Have** fruit in season.

Your purpose isn't out there somewhere, it's being cultivated in the soil of today.

This rhythm is something to remember as you journey through your seasons. It's helped me to be grounded, focused, and obedient.

Closing Thoughts

In this chapter, we discovered that **purpose is not what you do, it's who you're designed to be**.
It is the divine blueprint God embedded into your very being before you ever took a breath.

We distinguished **purpose from calling**:
Callings may shift across seasons, but purpose remains steady, it is the reason you exist.

We encountered the **Spirit of Might**, the divine force that strengthens your resolve, sharpens your courage and empowers you to act, not in your own strength, but in His.

We explored **Day Six of creation**, when God made humanity in His image and gave dominion to those formed in dust yet filled with His breath.
This day revealed that purpose is tied to identity and expressed through **responsible authority**.

Through the story of Moses, we saw that purpose can survive fear, failure and resistance.
All it takes is alignment: when identity, surrender and obedience meet, purpose is ignited.

Chapter 6: Purpose - Walking in Your Divine Design

Furthermore, I stopped chasing purpose like a prize to win,
And started trusting the One who planted it in me.
In surrender, purpose became peace—quiet, present, real.

Finally, we walked through the **BE–DO–HAVE model**, learning that divine purpose begins with becoming.
When you're rooted in who you are, what you do flows with clarity and what you have becomes fruit, not pressure.

Purpose is not performance.
It's permission.

The world may pull you in every direction,
But purpose will anchor you to God's direction.

You don't need a spotlight to walk in your design.
You just need **agreement**.
With your Creator.
With your calling.
With the quiet fire inside of you.

Let this be your pivot.
Your re-alignment.
Your moment of divine yes.

You were not created to drift.
You were formed to **walk with power**.

But even purpose must be held by something greater.
Even power must be rooted in purity.

The final Vine, **Love**, is not an accessory.
It is the reason.
The rhythm.
The root of it all.

Let's step into the most excellent way.
The Vine's crown.
And the heartbeat of the Kingdom.

Prayer Decreeing Purpose: Walking in Divine Purpose

I am not an accident, I am created with intention.

I am God's workmanship,
Created in Christ Jesus for good works
Which He prepared in advance for me to walk in *(Ephesians 2:10)*.
I was formed with purpose,
Fashioned in the image of God *(Genesis 1:27)*,
And called to walk in dominion, not fear.

I am filled with the Spirit of Might *(Isaiah 11:2)*,
Empowered to rise, to act, to build.
I do not shrink back. I do not drift. I do not wander.
I live with precision, authority and joy.

I walk in my divine design.
I don't chase titles, I follow truth.
My purpose is not defined by platforms or people,
But by the breath of God that called me into being.

I carry the courage of heaven.
I am strong in the Lord and in the power of His might *(Ephesians 6:10)*.
I am here on assignment.
I am marked by grace.
I am led by love.

I am not waiting to be validated,
I am already chosen *(1 Peter 2:9)*.

And every day I rise, I declare:
I will BE who He says I am.
I will DO what He gives me strength to do.
I will HAVE the fruit that comes from faithful stewardship.

Chapter 6: Purpose - Walking in Your Divine Design

This is not performance,
This is partnership.

In Jesus' name.
Amen.

This Is Love, Not Religion

Chapter 7: Love - The Crown That Holds It All

"Thus the heavens and the earth were finished, and all the host of them. And on the seventh day God ended His work which He had made; and He rested on the seventh day from all His work which He had made. And God blessed the seventh day and sanctified it: because that in it He had rested from all His work which God created and made."
(Genesis 2:1–3, KJV)

What Is Love?

Love is the very *nature* of God.

"God is love." (1 John 4:8, NIV)

This Is Love, Not Religion

It is who He is.
It's how He creates.
And it's why He sustains all things.

Love is not fragile.
It's not soft or passive.
It's fierce. Righteous. Intentional.

Love is alignment with heaven's standard,
The expression of God's will through selfless action.

But where love brings clarity,
Sin brings distortion.

Sin confuses.
Sin is missing the mark of God's standard.

Sin is separation.

It replaces devotion with indifference,
Vulnerability with fear,
Purity with lust.

Love is not confusion.
Love is *alignment*.

It gives you the strength to do what's right when it's inconvenient.
The courage to stay when walking away would be easier.
The grace to forgive when revenge feels justified.
The hope to endure when despair makes more sense.

As Joshua was reminded:

"Have I not commanded you? Be strong and courageous.
Do not be afraid; do not be discouraged,
for the Lord your God will be with you wherever you go."
(Joshua 1:9, NIV)

Chapter 7: Love - The Crown That Holds It All

When love is accepted, it flows in:
From the root of God's heart.
It grows strong within your soul.
And it flows outward, into every space you touch.

Love is not an emotion,
It is the platform upon which all emotions are rightly grounded.
It's the force that holds the entire framework together:

- **Boundaries** without love can harden into religion.
- **Identity** without love often swells into ego.
- **Animation** without love tends to be performance.
- **Management** without love risks becoming control.
- **Artistry** without love easily turns into self-glorification.
- **Purpose** without love slips into mere transactions.

Only love has the strength
To carry all the others, without breaking.

As Scripture so perfectly reminds us:

"Love is patient, love is kind.
It does not envy, it does not boast, it is not proud.
It does not dishonour others, it is not self-seeking,
It is not easily angered, it keeps no record of wrongs.
Love does not delight in evil but rejoices with the truth.
It always protects, always trusts, always hopes, always perseveres.
Love never fails."
(1 Corinthians 13:4–8, NIV)

But love isn't just an idea,
It's a *Spirit*.

To walk in love is to walk with *Him*.
To be rooted in love is to be filled with *His presence*.

Vulnerability allures transparency.
Transparency invites intimacy.

This Is Love, Not Religion

Intimacy builds understanding.
Understanding facilitates trust.
Trust builds confidence.
Confidence offers comfort.
Comfort gives rest.

And rest is where love lives.

Vulnerability is the gateway.
A position that belongs to the Lord only.
From there transparency is how we safely love others.

But before it can be shared with Him,
It must be honoured within.

To be vulnerable means to feel,
To sit with what's real
Instead of rushing past it
With adrenaline and distraction.

We often mistake movement for strength.
But sometimes,
That movement is just pride disguised as progress.

I say this not as a critic,
But as a witness to my own patterns too.

When we reject vulnerability,
We construct a version of ourselves
That love cannot reach.

It may look strong on the outside.
But it keeps intimacy at a distance.

And sometimes,
The very people who love us most,
Our mothers, fathers, and friends,
Are simply longing to witness our softness.

Chapter 7: Love - The Crown That Holds It All

Not to expose us,
But to love and be loved
In the best way they know.

This way of living
Is not what the world teaches.
But you weren't made to follow the world.
You were called to help heal it.
Because when we are vulnerable,
We are honest.

And honesty calls for truth.

And where truth is welcomed,
God draws near.

His Spirit cannot dwell
In spaces ruled by pride.

But the moment we agree with His light,
Something shifts.

We begin to shine too.

And the pride, shame, and darkness
That once ruled
Can no longer comprehend,
Or compete with the light.

Maybe this is your reset.

Not a forced surrender,
But a chosen one.

Not because life knocked you down,
But because you've chosen to kneel.

Let vulnerability be your daily posture,
Not just a painful interruption

This Is Love, Not Religion

When life humbles you,
But a rhythm of renewal.

Because strength is not the absence of weakness.
It's the courage to be seen.
To abide.
To let Christ meet you in your open place.
As Scripture says:
"Have I not commanded you? Be strong and courageous.
Do not be afraid; do not be discouraged,
for the Lord your God will be with you wherever you go."
(Joshua 1:9, NIV)

To be strong
Is to be soft before Him,
So that His strength can increase through you.

To be courageous
Is to walk by faith, not by sight.

And to win, truly win,
Is to carry a heart made clear
By Christ's love.
Let's meet the One who empowers it all,
The *Spirit of the Lord*.

The Rooted Spirit Manifested: The Spirit of the Lord

The *Spirit of the Lord* is not just a presence,
He is *power in communion*.

He is the breath of God
That brings intimacy without fear,
Holiness without shame,
And strength without striving.

Chapter 7: Love - The Crown That Holds It All

"The Spirit of the Lord will rest on Him—
The Spirit of wisdom and understanding,
The Spirit of counsel and might,
The Spirit of knowledge and the fear of the Lord."
(*Isaiah 11:2, NIV*)

He is the first Spirit listed.
The *root* from which all the others flow.

He is the voice in the garden saying,

"Where are you?" not because He doesn't know,
But because He wants to draw you near.

He is the *I AM*, the One who simply *is*.
He doesn't try to be present.
He *is* presence.
Fully. Faithfully. Freely.

"The Spirit of the Lord is upon Me,
Because He has anointed Me to proclaim good news to
the poor.
He has sent Me to bind up the brokenhearted,
To proclaim freedom for the captives
And release from darkness for the prisoners..."
(*Luke 4:18, NIV*)

This Spirit is not passive.
He binds, sends, frees, and heals.

That's why the Spirit of the Lord is the One who *empowers love*.
Because real love doesn't just feel, it *frees*.

He invites. He covers. He anoints.
He brings people close without crushing them.
He holds you, and still calls you higher.

This Is Love, Not Religion

His presence is not performance, it's *proximity*.
Not silence, it's *stillness*.
Not absence, it's *fullness*.

When love moves through the Spirit of the Lord,
It doesn't compete for attention.
It restores intention.

And in that sacred flow,
The soul rests.
The heart opens.
And love begins to *govern*.

His presence doesn't rush.
It doesn't strive.
It *rests*.

God is all-powerful, all-knowing, and ever-present.
Yet by nature, God does not coerce, but He reigns,
And at times intervenes according to His sovereign will.
He governs with love and manages with purpose.
His sovereignty doesn't override our will;
It orchestrates redemption like a symphony,
Each note purposeful, each movement led in grace.

He invites. He allows. He guides.

If He wanted robots, He would've made them.
Instead, He gives us choice,
Even if that choice leads to pain.

To call Him Lord is not to lose yourself,
But to return what was always His:
Your spirit, freely given, now freely surrendered.

Through faith and marked by baptism,
You enter the Kingdom's rhythm,
Where heaven's provision meets earth's assignment.
A life empowered. Set apart.
Not isolated from the world,

Chapter 7: Love - The Crown That Holds It All

But made whole within it.

And just as the Spirit of the Lord brings stillness to the soul,
God established a rhythm of rest in the very design of creation.

Let's step into Day Seven,
Where love teaches us not to perform,
But to *abide*.

Creation and the Seventh Day

"By the seventh day God had finished the work He had been doing; so on the seventh day He rested from all His work.
Then God blessed the seventh day and made it holy, because on it He rested from all the work of creating that He had done."
(Genesis 2:1–3, NIV)

On the seventh day, God didn't make anything.
He didn't separate or fill or form.
He didn't command or create.
He *rested*.

But He wasn't tired.
He was *satisfied*.

Love had spoken.
Order had come.
Creation had responded.

And so He blessed the space… and called it holy.

This was more than stillness.
It was alignment.
It was communion.

This Is Love, Not Religion

He didn't rest because He needed a break.
He rested because everything was in its place.

That's what love does.
It completes what striving never can.
It calls us not to do more, but to abide more deeply.

It's you, *being*...
Not *doing*,
In the Spirit of the Lord.

Love teaches us that rest isn't the absence of work,
It's the presence of God in everything we've built.

When you're rooted in love,
You stop rushing to prove.
You start moving from peace.

You live from a rhythm that heaven recognises.

Because the true evidence of divine love,
Is not loud... but lasting.
Not frantic... but full.

And there's no better picture of love-driven rest
Than Moses on the mountain.

He wasn't asking for victory.
He was asking for *presence*.

Let's enter that moment
Where love didn't just direct the journey,
It *defined* the destination.

Chapter 7: Love - The Crown That Holds It All

A Living Example: Moses Asks for Presence *(Exodus 33)*

Moses had seen miracles.
The Red Sea parted.
Bread fell from heaven.
Water flowed from rock.

He had experienced God's *power*,
But now he longed for His *presence*.

In *Exodus 33*, God offers to send an angel ahead to lead Israel into the Promised Land.
Victory was guaranteed.
The destination would be reached.

But Moses knew... it wasn't enough.

*"If Your Presence does not go with us,
do not send us up from here."*
(*Exodus 33:15, NIV*)

This was the language of love.

He didn't want the land without the Lord.
He didn't want promise without presence.
He didn't want progress without intimacy.

Love is not satisfied with results.
Love longs for relationship.

Moses wasn't asking God to move faster.
He was asking Him to stay *close*.

Because love doesn't rush.
It *rests*.
It *remains*.

This Is Love, Not Religion

This is what makes Moses a living example of divine love:
He didn't measure success by outcomes, but by *proximity*.

He knew what we must remember:
Without presence, nothing is worth building.
Without love, nothing is worth keeping.

But what happens when you believe in love...
Yet still feel dry?

When you're doing all the right things,
And yet, feel far from the closeness you long for?

Let's enter that space.
Where love feels just out of reach,
And grace is preparing to meet you there.

The Scenario: When You Love but Feel Empty

You're doing all the right things.

You've shown up.
You've served.
You've forgiven.
You've waited.
You've believed.

So why do you feel... **empty**?

Why does your soul feel quiet when your heart is loud?
Why does love feel more like labour than intimacy?

This is the tension no one talks about,
When your hands are full of good works,
But your soul still aches for connection.

Chapter 7: Love - The Crown That Holds It All

You're not bitter.
You're not lost.
But something feels distant... incomplete.

You wonder:
Is it me?
Is it Him?
Is it time to let go... or lean in?

But maybe, just maybe,
It's not distance at all.
It's an invitation.

An invitation to love differently.
To rest more deeply.
To stop loving from pressure
And start loving from **presence**.

Because love was never meant to be drained.
It was meant to **abide**.

And when you feel that subtle ache,
It's not proof you've failed.
It's proof that your soul remembers:
You were made for more than striving.

And sometimes,
That ache becomes a question.
A confrontation.

Where God doesn't just invite you to love,
He reveals where your love has been shaped
By pressure, not presence.

By proving, not abiding.

Before He showed me how love was meant to live in me,
He showed me how love was revealed in Him.

Let's return to the wilderness,

This Is Love, Not Religion

To the place where love refused to perform.

Chapter 7: Love - The Crown That Holds It All

My Turning Point: The Freedom of Being

1. Afraid of Being Seen

I was scared of love, outside of my family, it felt cold and Transactional.
It felt like something I needed to earn.

I knew people showed a form of love,
I felt I had to manufacture it,
Some relationships, friends and flings, felt cool but distant.
As if it was good for a season but I knew it wasn't deep.
A kind of going with the flow.

I wanted more but didn't want to be exposed.
To see me was too real, besides I wasn't confident in myself
So why would I allow myself to show myself.
So I guarded up.
The imaginary ego became my haven.
To be protected yet forever misunderstood.

This turned me into a liar,
I withdrew, cheated, cut off.
Alone.

---

2. What I Couldn't Give

I couldn't give what I didn't have.
And in the process, I hurt people.
Family. Friends. Past loves.
Wounds I caused...
Often unaware.
Often to myself.

It is right to say:
"Hurt people, hurt people."

This Is Love, Not Religion

It wasn't physical abuse.
But emotional erosion.
A slow leak of love through broken places.

---

3. The Collapse That Revealed the Root

It took a breakup,
A romantic collapse,
To finally confront my distorted view of love...
And lift my eyes to Christ.

---

4. Beholding Love, Becoming Whole

And as I began to behold Jesus more clearly,
I began to see myself more truthfully:
Indifferent.
Fearful.
Selfish.

Not beyond saving,
But in desperate need of it.

Everything changed When I began to see love the way **God sees it**:
Not something to strive for...
But something to receive.
And **become**.

---

5. Rest, Not Performance

God isn't waiting for us to impress Him.
He's not withholding affection until we get it right.

Chapter 7: Love - The Crown That Holds It All

He **is** love.
And His Spirit, the Spirit of the Lord,
Draws near not when we perform,
But when we **rest**.

---

6. A New Way of Seeing

I remember praying one day:
*"God, help me see people as You see them,
Or at least how You want me to see them."*

And slowly, something shifted.
He began to bring **order to my mind**.
A new way of seeing.

I found joy.
But not joy in achievement...
Joy in **being**.
In others being.

It felt strange at first.
But it was real.

---

7. Love Without Requirement

I began loving people without needing them to change.
Seeing beauty in difference.
Wanting to **protect identity**,
To help people guard their souls through love-shaped boundaries.

And I began to **hate** what threatened that being:
Lying.
Unforgiveness.

Comparison.
Performance.

---

8. The Rewiring of the Heart

God was **rewiring my heart**.
Not through a love I had to perfect,
But through a love I was simply invited to **participate in**.

I was humbled.
Because I saw how poorly we love.

And yet... God didn't demand flawlessness.
He simply asked me to try.
Not in my own strength,
But in His.

---

9. A Father's Kind Instruction

That's why He must be **Lord**,
Because only He can cover our gaps.

It reminded me of a child poorly helping their father:
The father doesn't reject the child for being unskilled.
He draws them in.
Teaches.
Corrects gently.
So they can learn... and become like Him.

That's love.
That's the Kingdom.

We love because He first loved us. (1 John 4:19, NIV)

10. Living From Presence

That revelation **set me free**.

I stopped being protected and distant.
And started living in presence of God
Which gives strength to love people courageously.

I realised:

When love becomes your motive,
Not just your reward,
Freedom enters the room.

---

11. A Love That Must Be Lived

But love, like anything alive, must be **tended**.
Not just felt. Not just known.
But **lived**.

Let's explore how love can be shaped in your daily life,
So it flows not from pressure,
But from the **freedom of being**.

Practicing Love in Daily Life

Making the Invisible Love of God Visible in Everyday Life

To live a life of love.
Consistently. Faithfully. Truthfully,
We need more than good intentions.
We need a framework.

Love flourishes within structure.
It grows when it's rooted in alignment.

This is the rhythm God follows in His own nature.
And it's the same rhythm we are invited to live by.

Here's how I've come to understand it:

The Foundation of Essence: The "Why We Do It"

Essence is the core, the unseen root that feeds every action.
It's not just why you do something.
It's why **God** does.

"God is love…" (1 John 4:8, NIV)

He disciplines because He loves.
He forgives because He loves.
He corrects, comforts and calls, because love is His essence.

When His "why" becomes your why,
Your motives shift.
You stop reacting from wounds and start responding from wholeness.

Your Practice:
Ask God to reveal His "why" behind how He loves.
Why do You wait? Why do You restore? Why do You bless?
Let that become the foundation of your own love rhythm.

The Frame of Principles: The "How We Do It"

Principles are timeless truths, anchors that don't change with circumstance.

Chapter 7: Love - The Crown That Holds It All

Love isn't a feeling first.
It functions by truth first.
It moves in righteousness, not recklessness.

"Love does not delight in evil but rejoices with the truth..." (1 Corinthians 13:6, NIV)

God's love operates on principles:
Sowing and reaping.
Grace and truth.
Freedom and obedience.

Your Practice:
Choose one area of life: Godliness, Mindset, Well-being, Family, Community, Work, or Wealth.
Ask: *"What principle is love calling me to uphold here?"*
Let God's Word shape your standards.

The Formation of Strategies: The "When and Why We Act"

Strategy is love in motion.
It's how we discern what love looks like in the **timing** and **context** of real life.

Sometimes love waits.
Sometimes it confronts.
Sometimes it says nothing.
Sometimes it says everything.

"There is a time for everything..." (Ecclesiastes 3:1, NIV)

Strategy is where wisdom and timing walk hand in hand.

Your Practice:
Pray: *"Holy Spirit, what is this moment calling for?"*

Listen before acting.
Strategy begins in stillness, then moves with clarity.

The Flow of Tactics: The "What We Do"

Tactics are the tangible acts.
The seen.
The felt.
The simple, sacred movements that reflect the heart of God.

It's not grand gestures, it's consistency.
Small obediences. Hidden mercies.
Daily love that makes heaven known.

Your Practice:
Ask, *"What small act can I do today that makes love visible?"*
A word of encouragement.
A moment of listening.
A gesture of grace.

These are not distractions.
They are discipleship in motion.

Chapter 7: Love - The Crown That Holds It All

THE FLOW OF DIVINE LOVE

Making The Invisible Love Of God Visible in Everyday Life

From divine identity to daily action.
From God's heart to our hands.

This Is Love, Not Religion

I was inspired by Dr. Myron Golden who used a version of this in business
But I saw something different,
A divine order that mirrors how God loves us.

Here's how divine love becomes lifestyle:

Essence gives birth to **Principles**
→ Principles inform our **Strategies**
→ Strategies reveal real-time **Tactics**

And when love flows in this order,
From unseen to seen,
From heart to habit,
It becomes more than a value.

It becomes a holy rhythm.
A way of living that reflects God,
Even in the hardest places.

Yet to know God is to be in His presence.

"Enter His gates with thanksgiving and His courts with praise..."
(Psalm 100:4, NIV)

Thanksgiving and praise are not just polite gestures,
They are keys.
They open the gates of heaven's presence.
They are spiritual access points that shift atmospheres and realign our hearts.

When we give thanks, we remind our souls of what is true.
When we praise, we exalt the One who is greater than what we feel.

Darkness feeds on despair and disconnection.
But gratitude draws us back to the Source.
Praise lifts our eyes above the storm.
It anchors us, not in our performance, but in His presence.

Chapter 7: Love - The Crown That Holds It All

In a world that wants us to strive, fight, and perform,
Thanksgiving is how we remain.
Praise is how we abide.
And love is the atmosphere we are drawn into when we do.

Because love is not just felt, it's entered.
And the gate is open to all who will thank Him.

Love as Sabbath: The Seventh Day Rest

On the seventh day, God rested.

Not because He was tired, but because the work was complete.
Creation wasn't finished with man, it was finished with rest.
And that rest wasn't absence, it was presence.
Love didn't come after the work.
Love was the rest in which the work was enjoyed.

This is the mystery of Sabbath.

More than a command it is an invitation.
More than a rule, it is a rhythm.
And Christ fulfilled it, not by abolishing rest,
But by becoming it.

He said, *"Come to Me… and I will give you rest." (Matthew 11:28, NIV)*
Not the kind you find in sleep, but in surrender.
Not the kind that waits for the storm to pass,
But the kind that walks on water in the middle of it.

To rest in Christ is to trust in His finished work.
To cast your burdens on the One who carried them.
To live, not in striving, but in stillness that moves with power.

The Vine is a picture of this rest.

This Is Love, Not Religion

Each pillar: Boundaries, Identity, Animation, Management,
Artistry, Purpose, Love,
Is not a ladder to climb,
But a pattern to follow.

You don't force fruit.
You tend the vine.

By focusing on boundaries,
God grows what's true,
From Boundaries to Love.

Because love is not earned by effort.
It's revealed in rest.

The Vine: A Life Rooted in Rhythm

Boundaries clear the false.
They protect what is sacred and reveal what doesn't belong.
They mark where you end and others begin,
making space for truth to rise.

Identity reveals the true.
Once the noise is quieted, you can hear the name God gave you.
No longer defined by past roles or wounds,
You recover who you were before the world told you to hide.

Animation brings identity into motion.
You stop performing and start expressing.
Your preferences, style, and presence begin to reflect who you really are,
Not as imitation, but as image-bearing.

Management gives your animation direction.
It channels your energy through order.
Desire meets discipline.
You begin to govern what God has given, not just feel it.

Artistry fills that structure with meaning.
You don't just build, you create.
Your life becomes a canvas for wisdom.
Expression becomes influence and beauty finds its place in design.

Purpose aligns it all.
You move from impact to intention.
No longer chasing tasks, you walk in assignment.
Your gifts serve something eternal, bigger than you, but made for you.

Love becomes the crown.
Not the reward, but the rhythm.
Not the start of the Vine, but the sign that everything else is rooted.
You no longer strive to love, you live from it.
Love becomes the atmosphere you carry and the legacy you leave.

Closing Thoughts

In this final Vine chapter, we discovered that **love is not just an emotion, it is the essence of who God is.**

It is where we see how love isn't a feeling; it is the foundation truth in which feelings arise from.

We began by exploring love as the **root** of everything God does. From creation to correction, from justice to joy, love is the motive, the method and the meaning.

We encountered the **Spirit of the Lord**, the first listed in Isaiah's sevenfold Spirit. He is not only present, He is **presence** itself. He brings freedom, intimacy and alignment, not through striving, but through communion.

Through the lens of **Day Seven of creation**, we saw that love does not always look like action, it often looks like **rest**. When everything God made was in order, He didn't keep working. He stopped. He blessed. He called it holy. In the rhythm of rest, love abides.

Moses showed us what it means to choose presence over progress. *"If Your presence does not go with us, do not send us."* That was the cry of love, a desire not for outcomes, but for nearness.

Then we walked through my personal story, how love became not something to earn, but something to embody. I discovered the freedom of **being** and from that place, began to love without fear.

We practised the rhythm of love through the **Essence → Principles → Strategies → Tactics** framework.
A blueprint for how to live love daily,
Not from pressure, but from divine partnership.

The Sabbath is not the reward for finishing the work, it's the rhythm that blesses the work. When we live in love, we move from rest, not toward it. We honour God not just by doing, but by delighting in what He has already done.

Finally, This is The Vine: A Life Rooted in Rhythm,

Where love isn't the final step, but the flow that confirms alignment.

Each pillar builds upon the last, until love becomes not just your crown,

but your cadence.

Because when love becomes your **why**,
Your life becomes an echo of His heart.

Chapter 7: Love - The Crown That Holds It All

Love is not loud.
But it never goes unheard.

It moves through silence.
Heals through presence.
Speaks through small acts of courage.

It is not always grand.
But it is always glorious.

It's not a transaction.
"I'll worship You if You give me breakthrough"
Love isn't bartering with God.
It's abiding in Him.

Love is the first fruit and the final flame.
The beginning of the Vine and the crown that completes it.

You were not just made to receive love,
You were made to **release it**.

So let love rule your rhythms.
Let it rewrite your reactions.
Let it restructure your relationships.
Let it refine your work.
Let it restore your soul.

Because love is not an accessory to faith,
It is the **evidence of God**.

And when everything else fades,
Love will remain.

Now that you've been rooted in the Vine,
It's time to walk through the **Seasons**.

Because fruit doesn't appear all at once.
It appears in time.
Through rhythm.
Through trust.

Let's discover how your life can flow in harmony
With God's appointed timing.

Prayer Decreeing Love: Living in Love

I am not here to perform for love,
I am here to live from it *(1 John 4:19)*.

I am not here to prove my worth,
I am already loved by the One who gave me worth *(Romans 5:8)*.

I receive the love of God as my root and my reason *(Ephesians 3:17)*.
I am patient, because He is patient *(2 Peter 3:9)*.
I am kind, because He is kind *(Ephesians 4:32)*.
I forgive, because He forgave me *(Colossians 3:13)*.

Love is not just what I do,
It's who I'm becoming *(1 Corinthians 13:13)*.

By the Spirit of the Lord,
I walk in truth, abide in rest and overflow in grace.

Love governs my boundaries.
Love flows through my identity.
Love animates my movement.
Love orders my life.
Love shapes my gifts.
Love fuels my purpose.

And love is my witness to the world.

In Jesus' name.
Amen.

Chapter 7: Love - The Crown That Holds It All

Part II

Chapter 8: Fruitfulness - Experiencing Growth

"This is to my Father's glory, that you bear much fruit, showing yourselves to be my disciples." (John 15:8, NIV)

The Garden of Becoming

Before there was fruit,
There was soil.

Before there was harvest,
There was a vine.

And before there was movement,
There was stillness.

Your life is a garden,
Not of performance, but of becoming.

This Is Love, Not Religion

Every word you've received,
Every boundary you've honoured,
Every truth you've carried,
Has been forming something beneath the surface.

Fruit is not proof that you tried harder,
It's evidence that you stayed connected.
To God.
To His rhythm.
To His rest.

*"Remain in me, as I also remain in you.
No branch can bear fruit by itself; it must remain in the vine.
Neither can you bear fruit unless you remain in me."*
(John 15:4, NIV)

This is the mystery of spiritual maturity:
You don't produce fruit by striving.
You produce fruit by **abiding**.

Because fruit is not a reward,
It's a **result**.

It's the outward sign of an inward alignment.
It's what happens when you live from the inside out.

So now, we pause.
And we turn our attention not to more effort,
But to more awareness.

What is your life producing?
Where is heaven becoming visible through you?
And what kind of fruit is forming in the garden of your life?

Before we look at the fruit that's in your life,
Let's start with the fruit God produces in you.

Chapter 8: Fruitfulness - Experiencing Growth

The fruit of the Spirit is the fingerprint of His presence.
It's what love looks like when it becomes visible.
Let's begin there.

The Fruit of the Spirit: What God Grows in You

You don't grow the fruit of the Spirit,
The **Spirit** grows it in you.

It's not your labour.
It's your **yielding**.

The fruit of the Spirit is not a personality profile.
It's not about being nice, passive, or agreeable.
It is the nature of Christ
Made visible in you
Through the power of His Spirit.

*"But the fruit of the Spirit is love, joy, peace,
forbearance, kindness, goodness, faithfulness,
gentleness and self-control.
Against such things there is no law."*
(Galatians 5:22–23, NIV)

This is not a checklist.
This is a **character map**.

It is the evidence that God is at work in your heart,
Forming not just behaviour, but being.

And this is the flow:

Love: The keyfruit

The motive behind every miracle.
The why behind every word.

Joy: Strength through delight

Not based on circumstance,
But rooted in unshakeable trust.

Peace: The stillness within the storm

Not the absence of conflict,
But the presence of confidence in God.

Patience: The pace of heaven

Depth to understanding.
Steadiness in waiting.

Kindness: The touch of grace

Compassion made visible.
Gentleness turned outward.

Goodness: Integrity in action

Righteousness lived out in the open.
A heart aligned with heaven's standard.

Faithfulness: Consistency in love

Staying true even when it's hard.
Being dependable in the unseen.

Chapter 8: Fruitfulness - Experiencing Growth

Gentleness: Power under restraint

Strength surrendered to compassion.
Correction wrapped in mercy.

Self-control: Spirit-governed strength

The ability to lead your emotions
Rather than be led by them.

A Ripening Toward Love

The fruit of the Spirit is not a staircase or a checklist.
It's a garden, where fruit may ripen in different seasons.
I like to see it as a ripening in stages to the pinnacle of love.
This isn't doctrine, but reflection.
Not a prescription, but a perspective.
A lens through which we can consider how the Spirit may shape us over time:

Self-control: Discipline is needed to surrender to the Spirit rather than the flesh.

Gentleness: Self-control tempers strength, making room for humility and compassion.

Faithfulness: A gentle heart becomes steady and trustworthy over time.

Goodness: Faithfulness overflows into consistent moral action.

Kindness: Goodness begins to show itself outwardly in compassion.

Patience: Kindness, when stretched by time or difficulty, becomes patience.

This Is Love, Not Religion

Peace: A patient heart rests, no longer driven by anxiety or control.

Joy: In the peace of the Spirit, joy naturally rises up.

Love: Finally, all of these culminate in divine love, the selfless, sacrificial, Christlike love that reflects God Himself.

Perhaps in your journey, love is already leading.
Or maybe, the Spirit is quietly building the foundation beneath it.

Either way, this path reminds us:
It is the same Spirit-born life,
the same fruit, grown from the same Vine.

Love as the Vine and the Fruit

Love is not only the first fruit named,
It is also the Vine that feeds the rest.

There is a love that is received,
The love that comes from abiding in Christ's presence.
It is the vine-love:
The source, the lifeblood, the divine flow that strengthens your soul.

And then there is a love that is formed,
The love that is grown in you,
Through pruning, abiding, and spiritual formation.
This is fruit-love:
The mature, courageous, Christlike love that shows up in life,
In patience, forgiveness, sacrifice, and truth.

One is the love that roots you.
The other is the love that reveals you.

Chapter 8: Fruitfulness - Experiencing Growth

One fills you from the inside.
The other flows outward as evidence.

Together, they complete the picture:
Love as the beginning and the becoming.
Love as the source of strength and the summit of surrender.

When we remain in the Vine,
We grow in the fruit.
And when the fruit matures,
It always points back to the Vine.

Because love is not just a virtue we practice.
It is the very presence of God becoming visible through us.

The fruit is not produced just through pressure.
They are cultivated through presence.

They grow when you remain.
They bloom when you obey.
They mature when you **surrender**.

So if you want to see more fruit in your life,
Don't start with your actions.
Start with your connection.

Abide in Him.
And let the Spirit do what only He can.

Now that we've looked at the fruit God forms in your soul,
Let's turn to the fruit that appears in your world.

Because spiritual growth isn't meant to stay hidden,
It's meant to show up in every domain of your life.

Let's explore the **seven fruits of life**,
Where heaven touches earth.

Not All Fruit Is Healthy Fruit

Unified Garden Parable

Before we explore the gardens of our lives,
Let us pause and walk through this one.

It is lush. Green. Alive.
At first glance, everything seems to be in bloom.

But look closer.
One tree bears fruit too quickly, ripened in unnatural heat.
Another is wide and tall, yet its roots barely touch the soil.
There's a vine twisting around others, choking them slowly,
its fruit bright but bitter to the taste.

Near the edge, a bush glitters with waxy fruit
That never softens, never feeds.
Beautiful. Impressive.
But lifeless.

And in the center, a tree planted by the stream.
It grows slowly. Quietly.
Its fruit takes time.
But when you bite into it, it nourishes something deep in you.
Peace. Wholeness. Truth.

This is the mystery of fruit.
Not all growth is healthy.
Not all fruit is good.
And not everything that appears fruitful
Was grown from the Vine.

So before you look at what your life is producing,
Ask this first:

Is what's growing in me coming from God's presence,
Or just my pressure?

Chapter 8: Fruitfulness - Experiencing Growth

Let's now walk the gardens of our lives,
And examine the fruit more closely.

The Fruits of Life: Where Heaven Touches Earth

The Fruit of the Spirit grows in us.
But the Fruits of Life grow **through** us.

They are the visible gardens,
Where love becomes action,
Where peace becomes presence,
And where God's truth becomes tangible.

These are not just areas of responsibility.
They are domains of divine evidence.
Each one holds the potential to reflect heaven,
When the Spirit is allowed to flow freely.

Let's walk through the seven Fruits of Life:
A framework for Spirit-formed living.

---

1. Godliness: Your Life with God

In one part of the garden stands a tree lit by lamps,
Always glowing but never growing.
It has been shaped for display,
Pruned to please onlookers,
But its roots barely touch living water.

Godliness is not the shine of performance.
It is the strength of presence.
It grows in hidden soil,
Nurtured by reverence and rooted in obedience.

This Is Love, Not Religion

Christ echoed godliness not by putting on a show,
But by constantly retreating to be with the Father.
He rose early to pray. He lived in alignment, not just appearance.
He said, *"I do nothing on my own but speak just what the Father has taught me."*
(John 8:28, NIV)

His life revealed this truth:
Godliness is not perfection, it is proximity.
It is walking with God until your life whispers His name.

Love and faithfulness take root here.
They steady your steps and deepen your desire to dwell in Him.

"Train yourself to be godly." (1 Timothy 4:7, NIV)

Check the Fruit:
Do I seek God's presence more than His blessings?
Does my life echo His nature even when no one is watching?

Chapter 8: Fruitfulness - Experiencing Growth

Godliness grows when three roots intertwine: **Bible study, prayer, and walking with God.**

If one is missing, we stumble: misguided steps, struggling with keeping commands, or striving in our own strength.

But when all three work together, they lead us into the steady presence of God, where true godliness takes shape.

BOUNDING TO GODLINESS

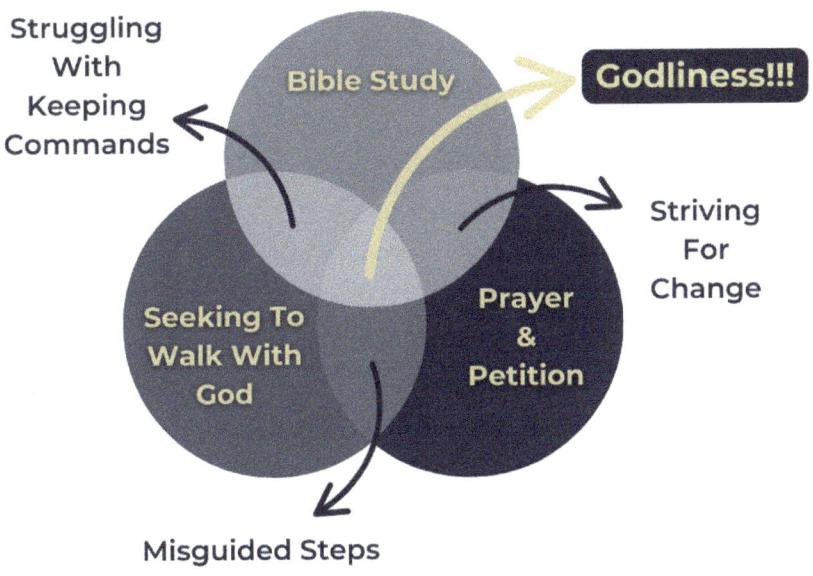

2. Mindset: Your Mind and Inner World

In the corner of the garden, there's a stream
That waters both flowers and weeds.
No one notices at first,
But over time, the weeds begin to choke the beauty,
Filling the space with noise, not life.

Your mindset is that stream.
If it flows with truth, it brings clarity.
If it's filled with fear, it multiplies confusion.

Mindset is the mindset of Christ.
It is the renewal of your thoughts
Until they move at heaven's pace
And rest in heaven's peace.

Christ echoed this fruit in every decision.
He did not react from fear, even under pressure.
When tempted in the wilderness, He responded with truth.
When faced with betrayal, He remained composed.
He said, *"Do not worry about your life..." (Matthew 6:25, NIV)*
And lived that freedom Himself.

His mind was governed by the Spirit,
And so His life flowed with unshakeable peace.

Peace and self-control help govern this space.
They bring clarity to your choices and stillness to your storms.

"Be transformed by the renewing of your mind." (Romans 12:2, NIV)

Check the Fruit:
Are my thoughts discipled by Scripture or driven by fear?
Is my mental space a sanctuary or a battlefield?

Chapter 8: Fruitfulness - Experiencing Growth

What we believe shapes how we think.
Our thoughts guide our actions.
Repeated actions form habits.
Habits shape our character.
Character defines our values.
And values give rise to hope.

Belief is the seed, but hope is the fruit.

HOW BELIEFS TURN TO HOPE

3. Well-being: Your Harmony Within

There is a tree in the garden that bears fruit all year round.
But its leaves are pale and its branches sag under the weight.
It never stops producing,
But it's slowly dying from the inside out.

Some fruit is grown without rest.
Some lives succeed without being whole.

Well-being is not self-indulgence, it is stewardship.
It is the alignment of spirit, soul and body
So that you can be fully present in your purpose.

Christ echoed this fruit by honouring the body He took on.
He rested. He withdrew. He wept. He ate.
He slept in storms, not because He didn't care,
But because He was secure in the Father's care.
He said, *"Come to me, all you who are weary… and I will give you rest."*
(Matthew 11:28, NIV)
And He modelled that rest in motion.

His strength wasn't frantic.
It was full of rhythm, grace, and trust.

Joy and gentleness help nurture this fruit.
They remind you that healing is holy
And rest is resistance to a world that never stops.

"Do you not know that your body is a temple of the Holy Spirit?" (1 Corinthians 6:19, NIV)

Check the Fruit:
Am I prioritising rest, reflection, and restoration?
Do I treat my body and emotions as sacred or secondary?

Chapter 8: Fruitfulness - Experiencing Growth

4. Family: Your First Circle of Love

There's a vine in the garden tangled with thorns.
It started strong, wrapping around others for support,
But now it pulls them down,
Its weight too heavy, its grip too tight.

Love was meant to lift, not control.
To cover, not consume.
Family can either be the soil where love grows deep,
Or the place where roots are cut too soon.

Family is the first classroom of love.
It is where honour is learned,
Where forgiveness is tested,
And where faith becomes flesh and blood.

Christ echoed this fruit in how He honoured His earthly parents,
Even as the Son of God.
He cared for His mother from the cross *(John 19:26–27, NIV)*,
And He called His disciples His brothers.
He corrected with compassion and protected with power.
He restored Peter after failure, not with shame, but with a meal.
He said, *"Whoever does the will of my Father... is my brother and sister and mother."*
(Matthew 12:50, NIV)

In Christ, family was never limited to blood,
It was widened by love and held together by truth.

Patience and kindness help hold this garden together.
They teach us to forgive quickly and honour deeply.

"But if anyone does not provide for his relatives... he has denied the faith." (1 Timothy 5:8, NIV)

Check the Fruit:
Is love expressed here through words and actions?
Am I present with my family, or just nearby?

---

5. Community: Your Circle of Influence

In one patch of the garden, the trees grow close together.
At first, it looks like unity.

But some stretch too far, stealing light from the rest.
Others shrink, their roots crowded, their growth stunted.

Community can either multiply strength
Or magnify imbalance.
It can sharpen character
Or silence it.

Community is where identity multiplies.
It is the soil where humility, correction, and celebration
Coexist in sacred tension.

Christ echoed this fruit in how He moved among people.
He walked with the broken. Ate with the outcast.
Served without a need to be seen.
He washed feet.
He embraced the lonely.
He called the overlooked by name.

He said, *"By this everyone will know that you are my disciples, if you love one another." (John 13:35, NIV)*

In Jesus, community was not just common interest,
It was covenant love made visible.

Goodness and gentleness blossom here.
They show up as humility, service,
And truth spoken in love.

Chapter 8: Fruitfulness - Experiencing Growth

"Carry each other's burdens..." (Galatians 6:2, NIV)

Check the Fruit:
Do I contribute to unity or disconnection?
Am I a safe place for others to grow?

---

6. Work: Your Calling in Motion

There is a tree planted near the edge of the garden.
Its branches are long and its harvest is heavy.
But the soil beneath is cracked.
The roots are dry.
It grew fast but not deep.
And now it groans under the weight of its own output.

Work can wear you down when it grows without worship.
It can become a stage for performance
Or a platform for purpose.
It can either reflect God's heart
Or replace His voice with hustle.

Work is not just labor.
It is love made visible through craft, service, and commitment.

Christ echoed this fruit in how He moved with purpose.
He built in silence for thirty years
Then fulfilled His calling in three.
He healed with compassion, not competition.
He said, *"My Father is always at His work to this very day, and I too am working." (John 5:17, NIV)*
But even He withdrew to rest and pray.

Jesus worked from fullness, not from striving.
His work flowed from identity, not insecurity.
And every act was rooted in love.

Faithfulness and goodness thrive here.

They turn tasks into testimony
And make your labor a light to others.

"Whatever you do, work at it with all your heart, as working for the Lord." (Colossians 3:23, NIV)

Check The Fruit:
Am I working from a place of purpose or performance?
Does excellence or exhaustion define my output?

---

7. Wealth: Your Resources and Reach

There is a tree by the river that bears no fruit.
Its branches are full of leaves
And its roots stretch wide,
But every time a blossom forms,
It holds it tight, never releasing.
What was meant to feed others,
Withers in its grasp.

Wealth is not how much you hold,
But how freely you give.
It is not measured in accumulation,
But in alignment with God's heart.

Wealth includes money, time, access, ideas, and influence.
And all of it is sacred.
God entrusts it not for pride,
But for purpose.

Christ echoed this fruit not in luxury,
But in generosity.
He multiplied what was small.
He shared what He had.
He said, *"It is more blessed to give than to receive."* (Acts 20:35, NIV)
And then He gave everything, including His own life.

Chapter 8: Fruitfulness - Experiencing Growth

Jesus was never owned by things,
But He always used them to reveal the Kingdom.

Self-control and faithfulness are key fruits here.
They ensure what you hold does not begin to hold you.

"Command them... to be rich in good deeds and to be generous and willing to share." (1 Timothy 6:18, NIV)

Check The Fruit:
Do I release what God gives, or restrict it?
Am I managing according to God's will or mine?

Each part of your life is a garden.
And in each garden, something is growing.

Some fruit feeds.
Some fruit fades.
Some fruit looks good but leaves you empty.
But the fruit that flows from the Spirit—
That nourishes. That multiplies. That lasts.

In Christ, we have not only a model,
But a Vine.
Not just a teacher,
But a source.

As you walk these seven gardens,
Do not measure by effort or applause.
Measure by alignment.
By presence.
By the quiet evidence that God is forming something holy in your everyday life.

Because where the Spirit flows,
Heaven grows.

Now, let us return to how to tend this garden,
Not with striving,
But with surrender.

Living the Fruits

These are not performance metrics.
They are **evidence of alignment**.
They are what happens when you don't just know the Vine,
But live from it.

Godliness roots your life.
Mindset renews your mind.
Well-being restores your soul.
Family refines your love.
Community stretches your grace.
Work channels your calling.
Wealth multiplies your impact.

And all of them…
Bear witness to the God who grows fruit through surrendered soil.

The Battle for Inner Ground

We do not fight for victory; we fight from victory. The battle already belongs to the Lord, and He has overcome. His glory is revealed through the fruits of our lives. Our trials and testings do not earn the win, but refine us to walk in His triumph and to steward the spoils of a victory He has already secured.

Before we talk about tending the garden, we must be honest about the battle for the ground itself.
Fruitfulness is not just threatened by external storms or barren seasons.

Chapter 8: Fruitfulness - Experiencing Growth

It is often contested within.

Anxiety and depression are two of the fiercest battles in this inner war.
They have an impact in the fruitfulness of our lives.
They do not always announce themselves loudly, but they quietly sap strength, blur vision, and choke hope if left unattended.

I'm no expert, but through observation I've noticed how both external and internal factors play a role.
The external environment, what the world teaches, what we accept, and how we filter it.
And the internal environment, what we feed our body and mind, the beliefs we anchor in, and the way we process what we carry.

Anxiety often rises as a measure of how we see ourselves.
It is the urge to control present and future outcomes through the filter of past experiences.
But here's the truth I've learned:
The more I align with Christ's identity, the more I can trust that the outcome belongs to Him.
And if the outcome is His, then the victory is His.
That frees me to simply do my best, while thinking bigger than myself, knowing the gospel and God's glory will be seen, not just my own will.

Depression, on the other hand, feels like withdrawing inward, compressed into a low state of being.
It is like searching for light in the dark until you no longer feel like looking.
But when I sense myself moving low, I fight by leaning into the opposite.
I watch comedy, because laughter is light.
I speak truthfully to God and to friends, because honesty breaks silence.
And I sing, even when I don't feel like it, because worship shifts the weight and awakens presence.

Ultimately, my trust is not in myself but in Him.
That is what helps me move from one state to another.
Because I no longer live for me.
As Scripture says, *"In His presence is peace and joy" (Psalm 16:11).*
To seek Him is to release control, to trust who I am in His hands, and to fight for the soil of my soul.

This is the battle for inner ground:
To guard the heart against shadows,
To resist the pull of despair,
To remain in the heavenly present state where the Spirit still breathes life.

And as I wrote these words, a message reached me: *Read Isaiah 55.*
A reminder that His word never returns empty.
That even in weakness, He is sowing.
That even in silence, He is working.

So fruitfulness is not about pretending you never feel anxious or depressed.
It is about refusing to let those states claim the soil of your heart.
To fight for the ground is to fight for the fruit.
And when you remain in Him, even the most fragile soil can still bloom again.

Tending the Garden: Fruitfulness as a Lifestyle

Fruit doesn't grow through force.
It grows through rhythm.
Through tending.
Through trust.

Chapter 8: Fruitfulness - Experiencing Growth

Even a garden that's been well-planted
Can wither if it's left unattended.

The same is true for your life.

The Fruits of the Spirit and the Fruits of Life
Don't flourish by accident,
They flourish through **intentional abiding**.

Because fruitfulness is not about momentum.
It's about **maintenance**.

Here's how you tend the soil of your soul,
So the Vine can keep flowing through your life.

---

1. Stay Present with the Gardener

The presence of God is not a bonus.
It's the source.
Without His nearness, our *"fruit"* becomes effort.
Our output becomes empty.

"Apart from Me, you can do nothing." (John 15:5, NIV)

Practice:
Pause before your day begins and ask:
"Lord, how are You tending me today?"
Then listen.

Fruit grows when the soil is soft.
And your heart stays soft when it stays surrendered.

---

2. Water What's Been Planted

The word of God is like rain,
It revives what's already there.

Sometimes your life doesn't need a new seed.
It needs fresh **watering**.

"As the rain and the snow come down from heaven... so is my word that goes out from my mouth." (Isaiah 55:10–11, NIV)

Practice:
Instead of chasing a new teaching,
Return to a verse God already gave you.
Read it. Sit in it. Speak it aloud.

Water it with prayer.
Watch it begin to grow again.

---

3. Endure the Pruning: Let Him Trim, You Trust

Not everything green is good.
Even healthy vines are cut back,
Not because they're failing,
But because they're fruitful.

Pruning is not punishment.
It's the Father's preparation for more.

"He prunes every branch that does bear fruit, so that it will be even more fruitful." (John 15:2, NIV)

Practice:
When it feels like things are being stripped away,
Pause and ask:
"Lord, is this pruning, or protecting?"

Chapter 8: Fruitfulness - Experiencing Growth

Then stay near.
Let the Gardener finish what He started.

Because sometimes, the deepest growth
Is the cuts you didn't choose, but trusted Him to use.

---

4. Rest in the Pace of Grace

God grows fruit in seasons.
Some days are for sowing.
Some are for watering.
Some are for watching.

Your job isn't to rush the harvest,
It's to remain in rhythm with heaven.

*"Let us not become weary in doing good,
for at the proper time we will reap a harvest if we do not give up." (Galatians 6:9, NIV)*

Practice:
Release the pressure to perform.
Choose to rest in trust, not in striving.
You are not behind, you are becoming.

Because in God's Kingdom,
Faithfulness always bears fruit.

You don't need to force fruit to prove your growth.
You simply need to stay connected.
To tend the garden of your soul.
And to let the Spirit do what only He can.

Because the clearest evidence of transformation,
Is not applause or perfection...

It's fruit.
And that fruit is already forming in you.

Let's close with that truth.

Closing Thoughts

This chapter began with a garden,
Not of striving, but of growing.

We learned that fruit is not forced.
It's formed.
By the Spirit.
In rhythm.
Through rest.

We explored the **Fruit of the Spirit**,
The nature of Christ made visible in us:
Love, Joy, Peace, Patience, Kindness, Goodness,
Faithfulness, Gentleness and Self-Control.

These are not behaviours to perform.
They are evidences of presence.
The outflow of abiding in the Vine.

Then we turned to the **Fruits of Life**,
Seven visible gardens where spiritual maturity takes shape:

- **Godliness**: where reverence becomes rhythm
- **Mindset**: where truth transforms thought
- **Well-being**: where rest and purpose align
- **Family**: where love is practised in real time
- **Community**: where identity grows together
- **Work**: where calling becomes service
- **Wealth**: where stewardship reflects the Kingdom

Each area is sacred.
Each one is a garden.
And each one becomes fruitful
When the Spirit is allowed to flow freely.

Chapter 8: Fruitfulness - Experiencing Growth

We then learned how to **tend the garden**,
By remaining present,
Watering the Word,
Welcoming pruning,
And resting in God's pace.

Because fruitfulness isn't found in performance,
It's found in presence.

So if you've come to the end of this journey wondering,
"Have I changed?"
"Has all of this made a difference?"

Here is the truth:

You don't need to force fruit to prove your growth.
You simply need to stay connected.

Look at your thoughts.
Your responses.
Your patterns.
Your prayers.

Even if the fruit is small,
It is there.
It is holy.
It is growing.

You are the proof that grace can grow anything.

Fruit doesn't grow in a straight line.
It grows in rhythm.
In cycles.
In seasons.

Some areas of your life will bloom in the sunlight,
Others will be buried in the dark.
But all are sacred.
All are part of the garden God is growing.

This Is Love, Not Religion

Because fruit needs more than soil.
It needs **timing**.
It needs **seasons**.

And just as God shaped your identity in the Vine,
And revealed His nature through your Fruits,
He now invites you to **trust the process of change**.

To let go of control.
To move with grace.
To grow through every season of your becoming.

Next, we step into the rhythm of God's timing,
Where even your winter has meaning,
And your spring is already taking root beneath the surface.

Let's learn to live in season.

Prayer Decreeing Fruit: A Life in Full Bloom

Father,

Thank You for being the Master Gardener of my soul.
Thank You for tending to what no one sees,
For pruning what no longer serves,
And for watering what You've planted in me *(John 15:1–2)*.

Help me to remain in You,
Not just in devotion, but in direction.
Not just on Sundays, but in every sacred ordinary moment *(John 15:4)*.
Teach me to trust Your process.
To delight in Your pace.
To rest while You grow what only You can *(Mark 4:26–28)*.

Let the fruit of Your Spirit be visible in my thoughts,
My decisions, my conversations, my work *(Galatians 5:22–23)*.

Chapter 8: Fruitfulness - Experiencing Growth

Let my life reflect the quiet strength of love,
The stillness of peace,
The power of patience,
And the witness of joy that cannot be shaken.
Lord, make me a tree planted by living waters,
Rooted deep, bearing fruit in season,
With leaves that do not wither *(Psalm 1:3)*.

I don't want to just know You.
I want to reveal You.

Let my whole life be a garden where Your glory grows.

In Jesus' name.
Amen.

Chapter 9: The Seasons - Embracing The Rhythm for Growth

"There is a time for everything and a season for every activity under the heavens." (Ecclesiastes 3:1, NIV)

The Wisdom of Seasons

If life had only one setting, we would never grow. But God, in His infinite love, designed life to move in seasons. Just like the earth turns and the tides shift, your soul, your purpose, your relationships and even your fruitfulness evolve through time.

This chapter is about learning to see, accept and align with the divine rhythm of your life. You may not always know the forecast, but you can always trust the One who commands the weather.

Chapter 9: The Seasons - Embracing The Rhythm for Growth

The Four Seasons of Growth

The Bible teaches us through the metaphor of seasons, not just climate, but a flow of purpose. In the natural, we see four key seasons:

- **Spring**: Vision, beginnings, sowing
- **Summer**: Work, development, consistency
- **Autumn:** Reward, harvesting, evaluation
- **Winter**: Rest, pruning, reflection

Each of these has a role in shaping us. Spring encourages faith. Summer demands endurance. Autumn calls for gratitude. Winter invites surrender.

But here's where the beauty deepens:

The Fruits Flow Through Seasons

Every area of your life - your godliness, your mindset, your well-being, your family, your community, your work and your wealth - will move through every season.

Not just once, but again and again.

Fruit grows like a planet orbiting a moving sun, circling in rhythm, yet always progressing with purpose. What begins in one season will deepen in the next. Some areas of your life will be in harvest while others are being pruned. And that is grace. That is balance.

Here's what that looks like:

Godliness

- **Spring**: You rediscover your hunger for God, study Scripture afresh.
- **Summer**: You establish consistent rhythms of worship, prayer and fasting.
- **Autumn**: You bear fruit, your life reveals His presence quietly.
- **Winter**: He prunes hidden idols, deepens reverence in the silence.

Mindset

- **Spring**: New hope enters your thought life.
- **Summer**: You practise renewing your mind daily.
- **Autumn**: You recognise strength within and patterns that bring peace.
- **Winter**: You face doubt or grief, but learn trust in the dark.

Well-being

- **Spring**: You commit to caring for your body, your pace, your peace.
- **Summer**: You maintain boundaries, healthy habits and rest.
- **Autumn**: Your pace slows down; your soul and body settle in rhythm.
- **Winter**: You slow down again to listen to your inner life.

Chapter 9: The Seasons - Embracing The Rhythm for Growth

Family

- **Spring**: Reconciliation begins. New patterns form.
- **Summer**: You nurture connection through communication and consistency.
- **Autumn**: You experience deeper trust, love and shared wins.
- **Winter**: There may be conflict, distance, or waiting, but growth is hidden beneath.

Community

- **Spring**: New friendships form, or you feel called back to connection.
- **Summer**: You show up regularly, serve, support, contribute.
- **Autumn**: You're sharpened, known and strengthened by others.
- **Winter**: You may withdraw to heal or reset boundaries and that's okay.

Work

- **Spring**: A new opportunity or vision opens.
- **Summer**: You put in the hours. You refine your craft.
- **Autumn**: Your effort bears fruit: results, recognition, momentum.
- **Winter**: You reassess. Maybe you rest. Maybe God reroutes you.

Wealth

- **Spring**: You develop fresh goals and healthier resource mindsets.
- **Summer**: You steward your resources, relationships, budget, invest.
- **Autumn**: You experience provision and overflow. You give freely.
- **Winter**: You scale back, reprioritise, or trust God in scarcity.

Your Personal Season

You might be in a spring where everything feels new and exciting, or a winter where it's hard to feel anything at all. Neither is better. Neither is worse. They are simply what's now.

Ask yourself:

- What season am I in?
- What is God doing in me here?
- What should I be letting go of?
- What is being planted?

Let these questions create space in you. Space for grace. Space for growth.

The Spiral of Spiritual Growth

We often imagine life as a circle, events returning, seasons repeating. But God's design is not merely circular; it's spiral. Like a double helix, the journey curves through spring, summer, autumn, and winter again and again, familiar paths, yet never quite the same. With each orbit, we're not just going around; we're being drawn upward. Every season revisited carries us higher, deeper, closer.

Chapter 9: The Seasons - Embracing The Rhythm for Growth

This is not repetition without purpose. It is **repetition with revelation**.

In nature, a vine climbs in spirals, ever higher. In biology, DNA carries life upward in its twin-spiral form. And in the Spirit, God forms us through patterns that evolve, not aimlessly, but intentionally. The same challenges return, but we face them wiser. The same blessings return, but we hold them more humbly.

As you pass through these seasons again, do not say, *"I've been here before."*
Say, *"I've been here, but I am not the same."*

Because when you walk with Christ, every cycle is also a step forward.
Every season is not just a time, it's a **turn upward**.

If life is a double helix of seasons, Scripture shows that God is the axis around which everything turns, and grace and truth are the twin strands that carry us forward - not just repeating, but becoming.

- **Grace** lifts us when we fall, forgives us when we fail and sustains when we cannot.
- **Truth** grounds us, aligns us, and reveals what must be refined.

They spiral together, not in opposition, but in harmony, turning through each season of life.

*"And we know that in all things God works for the good of those who love him,
who have been called according to his purpose."*
(Romans 8:28, NIV)

*"The Word became flesh and made his dwelling among us.
We have seen his glory, the glory of the one and only Son,*

who came from the Father, full of grace and truth."
(John 1:14, NIV)

So, let the seasons of your life turn, not in circles of despair or delay, but in spirals of divine design.

You are not just enduring change.
You are being formed by it.

Grace and truth are not merely qualities to seek, they are the twin strands by which your life is being written, one season at a time.

And God, the unshakable center, is leading, lifting and helping you upward through every turn.

You are not stuck.
You are orbiting forward.
Not just repeating.
Becoming.

Practicing Seasonal Awareness

Here's how to live in harmony with the season you're in:

- **In Spring**: Start. Take small, obedient steps. Don't rush the bloom.
- **In Summer**: Be faithful. Stay rooted. Water what's working.
- **In Autumn**: Harvest joyfully. Reflect. Give thanks.
- **In Winter**: Rest deeply. Grieve honestly. Be still and know.

Chapter 9: The Seasons - Embracing The Rhythm for Growth

Closing Thoughts

Growth is not always visible.
But it is always happening.

You've walked through the Vine.
You've tasted the Fruit.
And now you're learning the rhythm of **when** and **how** things grow.

Seasons are not signs of success or failure.
They are signs of movement.
God's calendar is not marked by clocks, but by transformation.

There is a time to begin and a time to be still.
A time to plant and a time to prune.
A time to be hidden and a time to be seen.

And in each of these moments, God is present,
Not rushing you.
Not abandoning you.
But maturing you.

Because your life is not a static display of potential.
It's a living, breathing timeline of divine grace.

You are being shaped by a holy rhythm.
Not for perfection,
But for alignment.

Let every season teach you.
Let every delay refine you.
Let every shift be sacred.

You're not behind.
You're being prepared.

As we bring this journey to rest,
Let's seal what has been planted.

Let's honour the shifts.
Let's commit to remain faithful, no matter the season.

Because when you walk with God,
Even your winter carries the scent of spring.

Prayer Decreeing Seasons: Rooted in Every Season

Lord,

You are the God of every season (Ecclesiastes 3:1).
You know when to begin.
You know when to wait.
You know when to prune.
And You know when to bloom (John 15:2).

Teach me to trust Your timing (Psalm 31:15).

To release what I can't control (Proverbs 3:5–6).
To embrace what You're revealing in this moment.

Help me not to rush through the quiet seasons.
Or despise the hidden ones.
But to find You in all of them (Jeremiah 29:13).

When I'm tempted to measure progress by results,
Remind me that abiding is success.
That faithfulness is fruit.
That becoming is a process.

Give me wisdom in winter.
Joy in spring.
Strength in summer.
Vision in autumn.

Chapter 9: The Seasons - Embracing The Rhythm for Growth

Shape me not according to the world's pace,
But by Your eternal rhythm.

Let my life move with You,
In rest, in work, in wilderness and in wonder.

In every season,
Let me remain rooted in You.

In Jesus' name.
Amen.

Chapter 10: Becoming in the Kingdom of Light

"For you were once darkness, but now you are light in the Lord. Live as children of light…"

(Ephesians 5:8, NIV)

Kingdom Culture: The Boundaries That Protect What's Pure

Boundaries set the thermometer for culture.
Culture shapes the vision of humanity.
And vision reflects the image we chase,
The life we believe we should live.

But what happens
When the image is distorted?
When the culture is diseased?

Chapter 10: Becoming in the Kingdom of Light

I see cancerous nations,
Societies devouring themselves
In the name of progress.
Growth that eats through the soul,
Destruction laid as our foundation.

We've become hard-hearted.
Our values, delusional.
Functioning in pain,
Ignoring the aches of body and soul,
Refusing the healing.
Crying for release,
But clinging to control.
Desiring change,
But resisting transformation.

We have grown weak in strength,
Soft in will.
We long for good things (freedom, healing)
Yet choose wealth over wholeness.

We lie to ourselves
And call it self-awareness.
We distract ourselves with noise,
Conversations, entertainment, busyness,
That pacify, but never cure.

We've traded backbones for victimhood.
Entitlement has bred pleasures
That destroy what we pretend to protect.

We've normalised the slow killers like:
Smoking.
Processed food.
Pornography.
Overmedication.

Even music, meant to lift,
Has become a drug

This Is Love, Not Religion

When we use it to drown out reality
And manufacture delusion.

This culture reveals what we truly worship:
Selfishness.
Lies.
Pride.

We have made an altar to the enemy, the devil,
And called it freedom.

But the Kingdom speaks a different culture.
It is quiet.
Strong.
Healing.

Its values are:
Humility.
Truth.
Selflessness.

Our flesh is not just weakness,
It is rebellion in disguise.

As Dr. Dharius Daniels puts it:

"The flesh is a nature that rebels against God's design...
There's something wrong when I allow my flesh to drive my humanity...
Being angry is human, sinning out of anger is flesh.
Being hungry is human, being greedy is flesh."

The Kingdom calls us higher,
To godliness.
To responsibility.
To live with excellence,
Because that is who we are.

So rich in truth
That our boundaries stand fortified,

Chapter 10: Becoming in the Kingdom of Light

Holding corruption at bay.
Protecting what is pure.

We were born into a kingdom of deceit,
A culture that numbs,
That blinds,
That strips away identity
And replaces it with emptiness.

But we are called to a better Kingdom.
One not of this world,
But from above,
To overrule our low ways
And destined to transform it.

Heaven's rule on earth.
A Kingdom stronger than our pain,
Wiser than our wounds.

A Kingdom of,
Forgiveness.
Restoration.
Generosity.
And above all, love.

That's culture.

Jesus came to usher us in,
To call us ambassadors of heaven.
To give us authority,
Diplomatic immunity,
If we will yield.

But to live as Kingdom people,
We must know our King.
Be His people.
Walk in His principles.
Let every space (heart, home, habit)
Be His.

This Is Love, Not Religion

To do this,
We must let go.
Shed the false identity
This world has wrapped us in.
Let the identity of God rise in us.

How?
We surrender.
We give up our independence.
We ask Him to be our Lord and King.

Then we are born again,
Not only baptised into water,
But into a new way of being.

As heaven's ambassadors,
We walk in the authority of Christ.
Not just doing good,
But being light.

In Christ,
Transformation begins.
By the Spirit,
We face our fears,
Heal our pain,
And tell the story of why it was worth it.

We all choose a struggle:
A hard life without God,
Or a redeemed one
With peace, purpose, and joy
Even in the storms.

And yes, this world is getting darker.
Good.

Because the darker it gets,
The brighter the light will shine.

Chapter 10: Becoming in the Kingdom of Light

And before this world corrupts itself beyond return,
Jesus will come
And bring everlasting change.

What you just read is more than reflection,
It's a revelation.

The state of our world reveals the consequence of life without boundaries.

But now that we see it clearly,
What do we do?

If culture is shaped by vision,
And vision by what we value,
Then we must practice boundaries that reflect Heaven,
In how we think, live, speak, and serve.

Not just once.
Not just when it's easy.
But daily.

The Beatitudes: Becoming a Light in the Kingdom

"Now when Jesus saw the crowds, He went up on a mountainside and sat down. His disciples came to Him, and He began to teach them. He said:"
(Matthew 5:1–2, NIV)

We were never made to shine on our own. Like the moon reflects the sun, our calling is not to produce light, but to receive and reveal it. The Beatitudes are not just a list of virtues or blessings, they are sacred invitations into deeper formation. And the deeper that formation goes, the more clearly Christ's light is reflected through us.

Each movement into these words from Jesus is like turning a diamond in the light, another facet catches the sun. Another angle reveals His beauty. But this light is not abstract. It is meant to fill real places in our lives: our thoughts, our relationships, our pain, our decisions, our sense of purpose.

To walk in the Beatitudes is not to climb a ladder, but to descend, to bow lower in spirit, deeper in trust, wider in mercy. In every area of life where we humble ourselves, we make room for the Kingdom to enter and for the radiance of Christ to shine. What we surrender, He fills. And what He fills, He illuminates.

Beatitude I: The Poverty of Spirit

The deeper the soul bows, the more space there is for divine light to fill it.

"Blessed are the poor in spirit, for theirs is the kingdom of heaven."
(Matthew 5:3, NIV)

This is the gate to all other gates. The Kingdom of Heaven is not given to those who think they can manage life on their own. It belongs to the inwardly lowly, those who know that without God, they are bankrupt.

To be poor in spirit is to crouch low in the heart. It is to relinquish self-will so that the will of the Father can reign. This is why Jesus begins here: Heaven cannot fill a soul that is already full of itself.

Chapter 10: Becoming in the Kingdom of Light

Beatitude II: Those Who Mourn

Where the heart breaks open, mercy seeps through like morning rain on cracked ground.

"Blessed are those who mourn, for they will be comforted."
(Matthew 5:4, NIV)

Once the heart is humbled, it becomes tender, aware of all that is not right in the world and within the soul. This awareness is not sterile or cold; it stirs grief. We mourn not only for our sin, but for the suffering around us, for the brokenness that saturates our world, and for the distance between what is and what should be.

But this mourning is not hopeless despair. It is a holy ache, a longing for heaven's nearness in a fallen world. And in this longing, Christ promises comfort. Not always in the way we expect, but in the steady, sustaining presence of His Spirit. Mourning clears the fog of self-reliance and into that clear air, the light of divine compassion begins to shine.

Where we allow our hearts to break, the light breaks through.

Beatitude III: The Meek

The hands that surrender control become the vessels God entrusts with power.

"Blessed are the meek, for they will inherit the earth."
(Matthew 5:5, NIV)

True mourning cultivates a softness that leads to meekness. To be meek is not to be passive or weak, it is to be strong enough to stay surrendered. It is the quiet power of a soul that trusts God more than it trusts itself. The meek do not grasp, defend, or dominate. They wait. They yield. They walk in a strength the world cannot understand.

Meekness is not about giving up your place, it's about giving up your control. And paradoxically, those who release control are the ones entrusted with more. The earth is not inherited through force but through faithfulness. What we once tried to take by force, God now gives to the meek in His timing.

Meekness allows the light of Christ's authority to be revealed not through dominance, but through divine restraint and trust.

Beatitude IV: Those Who Hunger and Thirst for Righteousness

The soul that aches for heaven becomes a hearth where holiness makes its home.

"Blessed are those who hunger and thirst for righteousness, for they will be filled."

(Matthew 5:6, NIV)

Meekness creates space. And in that space, hunger grows. Not for power or recognition, but for righteousness. For God's justice, His truth, His holiness, His way. When we no longer need to fight for ourselves, we begin to crave something greater: His will on earth as it is in heaven.

This is not a passing craving, it's a holy ache. A thirst that no earthly success or pleasure can quench. To hunger for righteousness is to long for the world to be set right, starting with our own hearts. And that longing does not go unanswered. Christ promises: filling is not the reward of striving, it is the result of aligning. As our desires bend toward heaven, heaven fills us. And the light of Christ begins to blaze, not only around us, but within us. Righteousness becomes the

Chapter 10: Becoming in the Kingdom of Light

flame that purifies, directs, and defines the life of those who seek Him.

Beatitude V: The Merciful

The one who kneels to lift another stands tallest in the Kingdom.

"Blessed are the merciful, for they will be shown mercy." (Matthew 5:7, NIV)

Righteousness reveals both the holiness of God and the helplessness of man. As we hunger for what is right, we are confronted with the reality that we cannot attain it on our own. And in that realisation, grace becomes not just a gift, it becomes our lifeline.

Mercy is born from this place. When we know the depth of the mercy we've received, it becomes impossible to withhold it from others. Mercy is not weakness. It is strength restrained by compassion. It sees brokenness in others and chooses forgiveness over vengeance, compassion over judgment.

To be merciful is to live open-handed in a world that clings to debts and demands justice on its own terms. But mercy rewrites the rules. It releases others from what they deserve because we ourselves have been released.

In a world of harsh light and hard hearts, mercy softens and warms. It is the light of Christ bending low, reaching through us to heal what law alone could never touch.

Beatitude VI: The Pure in Heart

When your heart is no longer divided, the eyes begin to see the invisible.

"Blessed are the pure in heart, for they will see God."
(Matthew 5:8, NIV)

Mercy cleans the lens of the soul. When we live in grace, receiving it, giving it, our hearts are no longer clouded by judgment, pride, or self-justification. Purity of heart is not sinlessness; it is singleness of desire. It is a heart undivided, directed wholly toward God.

This purity refines not just what we do, but why we do it. It filters our motives, clarifies our intentions, and focuses our vision. The pure in heart are not distracted by lesser loves, they long to see God, and in that longing, they *do*.

Not just in eternity, but here. They see Him in beauty, in brokenness, in silence, in Scripture, in the face of the stranger. Their hearts become mirrors, reflecting His presence, even in a dim world.

As the heart becomes pure, the light becomes clearer. And in that clarity, God is no longer a concept. He is seen. Known. Felt. Followed.

Beatitude VII: The Peacemakers

Those who carry God's presence become bridges where heaven walks into broken places.

"Blessed are the peacemakers, for they will be called children of God."
(Matthew 5:9, NIV)

Chapter 10: Becoming in the Kingdom of Light

To see God is to be changed by Him. And those who are changed by Him cannot help but carry His likeness into the world. Peacemakers are not merely peacekeepers, those who avoid conflict. They are carriers of a higher order, stepping into chaos with heaven's truth and heaven's grace in hand.

Peacemaking is active. It costs something. It requires courage, humility, and a heart tuned to the heartbeat of the Father. These are not people who ignore brokenness, but those who walk into it with redemptive intent. They mend what's torn, bridge what's divided, and speak light into darkness.

To make peace is to align the earth with the rhythm of heaven. It is to bring what *is* into agreement with what *should be*. And when we do this, we are not simply acting like God's children, we are recognised as such. The family resemblance is clear. The Father's light shines unmistakably through them.

They do not just reflect Christ, they *embody* His mission.

Light That Cannot Be Hidden

When light is costly, it shines all the more clearly in the face of resistance.

"Blessed are those who are persecuted because of righteousness, for theirs is the kingdom of heaven."
(Matthew 5:10, NIV)

He ends where He began. The Kingdom. But now, the blessing is not only for those who are poor in spirit, it is for those who are **persecuted for what they've become.** When you carry the light of Christ, it will confront the darkness around you. The flesh does not welcome the Spirit. But even in the rejection, the Kingdom is yours. You belong to another world, and that world belongs to you.

Jesus closes this teaching with a charge:

This Is Love, Not Religion

"You are the salt of the earth... You are the light of the world... Let your light shine before others, that they may see your good deeds and glorify your Father in heaven."
(Matthew 5:13–16, NIV)

So this is how we shine. Not by skipping the process, but by walking through each phase of formation. These beatitudes are not behavioural checklists. They are **the becoming of a disciple**.

To be the light is not to be loud.
It is to be **lit**, with the flame of heaven.

Let your spirit be humbled,
so that His Spirit may rise.

Let your light shine.

Prayer of Becoming: Form Me by the Beatitudes

Jesus,
You climbed the mountain to speak,
not just to the crowds, but to the hungry-hearted *(Matthew 5:1–2)*.
Today, I sit at Your feet.
Speak to me. Shape me. Shine through me.

I do not want to only learn Your words,
I want to live them.
Let the Beatitudes form me from the inside out.

Make me poor in spirit,
so I can be rich in You *(Matthew 5:3)*.
Break the pride that blinds me.
Give me eyes to see heaven's Kingdom
as my true inheritance.

Chapter 10: Becoming in the Kingdom of Light

Teach me how to mourn,
To feel what You feel,
To grieve with hope,
To be comforted not by distraction
but by Your Spirit *(Matthew 5:4)*.

Clothe me in meekness,
Silence the war of my will.
Let obedience be my strength
and patience my posture *(Matthew 5:5)*.

Cause me to hunger and thirst for righteousness,
Let my cravings be sanctified.
Redirect every misplaced desire
until all I want is what pleases You *(Matthew 5:6)*.

Make me merciful,
not just in action, but in attitude.
Teach me how to forgive,
how to see others with Your eyes,
and how to carry grace without condition *(Matthew 5:7)*.

Purify my heart,
Refine my motives.
Burn away the mixture.
Let my intentions be clean
so that I may see You,
in the stillness, in the struggle, in everything (Matthew 5:8).

Anoint me as a peacemaker,
Not one who avoids conflict,
but one who carries Your presence into it.
Let me sow reconciliation,
and walk as a child of God in every place of division *(Matthew 5:9)*.

And if I am rejected for walking in this way,
Strengthen me.
Remind me that the Kingdom is mine.
Remind me that You were rejected first *(Matthew 5:10–11)*.

This Is Love, Not Religion

And remind me that the light You've placed in me
is not meant to be hidden.

Form me.
Fill me.
Shine through me.

In Your name I pray,
Amen.

Chapter 11: The Kingdom Invitation: Coming to Christ, Dying to Self, and Rising in New Life

"Come to me, all you who are weary and burdened, and I will give you rest.

Take my yoke upon you and learn from me, for I am gentle and humble in heart,
and you will find rest for your souls.
For my yoke is easy and my burden is light." (Matthew 11:28–30, NIV)

This chapter is for anyone longing for true freedom, peace, and a deeper connection to the source of life. Whether you're exploring faith for the first time, turned away from the faith or have walked with Christ for years, this message offers a fresh call to surrender, rest, and receive the fullness of life in Him. There is something here for the new believer and nourishment for the faithful too. Some truths are echoed more than once,

This Is Love, Not Religion

not to be redundant, but to help shift our perspective and sink deeper into the heart.

The world teaches us to hold on.

Hold on to control.
Hold on to identity.
Hold on to the illusion that we are enough on our own.

But the more we hold on, the more we rely on our own strength.
And the more we rely on our own strength... the further we drift from true rest.

How can you be free if you're still gripping the very thing that's holding you back?

God invites you to **let go of your life**, not to lose it, but to **receive true life in Christ.**

We all want good things: peace, joy, consistency, discipline.
But we chase them through performance, pressure, and perfection.
We try to earn what was always meant to be received.

And yet, we are human *beings*.
Not human *doings*.

Like orchids, we are designed to thrive... but only in the right environment.
The Holy Spirit is that environment.
Through Him, we receive the life of Christ.

Not by striving.
But by surrender.
Not by doing.
But by *being* in Him.

Chapter 11: The Kingdom Invitation: Coming to Christ, Dying to Self, and Rising in New Life

Why Jesus Had to Die—and Rise Again

When humanity was first born, it was when God breathed His Spirit into us. We were made to live in harmony with Him (heart, soul, mind, and strength) reflecting His image and likeness. To do this, we had to be holy as He is holy.

But we became unholy when Adam and Eve listened to the serpent in the garden. That first act of sin caused separation from God and broke the union between God's Spirit and human spirit. From then on, all were born of flesh, not Spirit.

To preserve us from eternal separation, God allowed humanity to live on earth, but with the hope of redemption. In the Old Testament, sins were temporarily cleansed by animal sacrifices, pure, innocent offerings of blood. But these were only shadows of a greater reality to come.

Jesus came as both fully God and fully man, born without sin. Though rich in Spirit, He made Himself poor (choosing humility) to show us that we, too, can walk in step with the Spirit of God. The Spirit fell upon Him as a sign that the way back to divine relationship had begun. He was the only one worthy to be the final sacrifice. To restore the union between God and humanity, Christ had to die, a pure and innocent offering, to cleanse not just the flesh, but the *spirit*.

"If Christ has not been raised, your faith is futile; you are still in your sins."
(1 Corinthians 15:17, NIV)

Through His resurrection, Jesus became the firstborn of a new creation, making a way for us to be born again. By this, He made it so we are covered by Him so that we can sit next to the Father with Him. This is the heart of the gospel:

"If you declare with your mouth, 'Jesus is Lord,' and believe in your heart that God raised him from the

dead, you will be saved."
(Romans 10:9, NIV)

The Gospel of the Kingdom of God

There is a Kingdom,
Not built by human hands,
Not ruled by earthly power,
But established before time by the eternal King: Jesus Christ.

But what is a kingdom?

A kingdom is more than a place.
It is a realm under the rule of a king,
Where his will is law,
His values shape culture,
And his people reflect his reign.

A true kingdom has five essentials:
A king who governs,
A people who belong,
A law that orders life,
A territory where authority is exercised,
And a culture formed by the heart of the ruler.

The Kingdom of God is no different,
Except that it is unlike any kingdom of this world.

This Kingdom has a King,
Not elected, but enthroned by divine right.
Jesus is not merely a teacher or prophet;
He is the Son of God, the image of the invisible God,
Sent to reconcile all things to the Father.

He rules not by force, but by truth, grace, and justice.
His sceptre is righteousness.
His first crown was a cross.

Chapter 11: The Kingdom Invitation: Coming to Christ, Dying to Self, and Rising in New Life

This Kingdom has citizens,
Not slaves, but sons and daughters.
Not perfect, but purified.
Those who were once far off are now brought near,
Adopted, awakened, and anointed to live as children of God.

This Kingdom has laws,
Not written merely on stone,
But engraved on surrendered hearts.
Its law is love.
Its standard is holiness.
Its source is the Word of God.

This Kingdom has territory,
Not confined to land,
But present in hearts, homes, cultures, and nations.
It spreads invisibly through faith,
And visibly through transformed lives.

This Kingdom has a culture,
Built not on the ways of the world,
But on the values of Heaven:
Righteousness, peace, joy in the Holy Spirit.
A kingdom of honour, truth, mercy, and self-control.
Where justice flows, humility is treasured,
And love is the highest aim.

But to enter this Kingdom,
Something must first die.
And something must be born.

This is why Jesus came, not only to forgive our sins,
But to transfer us from the domain of darkness
Into the Kingdom of light.

We are called to repent,
Not just of bad behaviour,
But of unbelief, pride, and self-rule.

This Is Love, Not Religion

We are called to trust the King,
Even when we do not fully understand.
To surrender to His authority
Is to walk into true freedom.

Jesus' life, death, and resurrection
Were not just historical events.
They were divine declarations:
That the King has triumphed.
Sin is defeated.
New life in the Spirit is possible,
For all who believe.
Death has lost its sting.
The door to the Kingdom is now open.

To follow Jesus is to die to sin
And rise with Him into new life.
Just as the King was raised in power,
So are we raised into a new way of being.

And this is the invitation:
To enter the Kingdom of God
Through spiritual rebirth.

We are born again,
Not of flesh, but of the Spirit.
Through repentance, belief, baptism,
And receiving the Holy Spirit,
We become living temples, bearing Heaven's light.

The Spirit doesn't come to visit.
He comes to dwell.
To guide us.
To transform us.

And there will be fruit,
Not forced, but flowing.
Love, joy, peace, patience, kindness, goodness, faithfulness,
gentleness, and self-control.

Chapter 11: The Kingdom Invitation: Coming to Christ, Dying to Self, and Rising in New Life

Not just personal change,
But Kingdom evidence.

This Kingdom is present now,
But one day it will come in fullness.

Jesus will return.
Not as a suffering servant,
But as conquering King.

Every knee will bow.
Every tongue will confess.
And the earth will be filled
With the knowledge of the glory of the Lord
As the waters cover the sea.

He will make all things new:
A new Heaven, a new Earth.
The Kingdom of God,
On earth as it is in Heaven.

You are invited.

Not when you've figured it all out.
Not once you've become perfect.
But now.
The King is calling.

Turn. Believe. Be reborn.
Live in the Kingdom of God,
And join the renewal of all things.

Receiving the Holy Spirit: The Return of Divine Breath

When Jesus was baptised by John, He had no sin, but He was showing agreement with the kingdom message. The Holy Spirit came *upon* Him, enabling Him to live out the fullness of Isaiah's prophecy about the Seven Spirits of God.

But the Spirit moved *within* Him when He breathed on His disciples saying:

"Receive the Holy Spirit."
(John 20:22, NIV)

We lost the Spirit through sin. But in Christ, we are made worthy to receive Him again.

To be born of the Holy Spirit, we must:

- Believe in Jesus as Lord and Saviour
- Be baptised in water, as water cleanses the spirit
- Be gifted and filled with the Spirit by your faith in Jesus Christ

This is not symbolic, it's spiritual rebirth.

What You Must Do

"Repent, and be baptised every one of you in the name of Jesus Christ for the remission of sins, and you shall receive the gift of the Holy Spirit."
(Acts 2:38, KJV)

Chapter 11: The Kingdom Invitation: Coming to Christ, Dying to Self, and Rising in New Life

Here's the sacred order:

1. **Repent**: Turn away from sin and turn toward Christ.
2. **Believe**: Receive Him as Lord and Saviour, trusting His finished work.
3. **Be baptised**: Enter into death and resurrection through water.
4. **Receive the Holy Spirit**: Invite His Spirit to dwell within and rule over your life.

You were not made to strive.
You were made to be *filled*.

You were not made to perform.
You were made to *be fruitful*.

You were not made to die in the flesh.
You were made to *live by the Spirit*.

"Taste and see that the Lord is good."
(Psalm 34:8, NIV)

Baptism: The Death that Brings Life

We saw it foreshadowed in the Old Testament. In Leviticus 6:13, the fire on the altar was never to go out. Sacrifice was constant, a continual offering before God.

Now, we are the altar.

"Present your bodies as a living sacrifice, holy and pleasing to God, this is your spiritual worship."
(Romans 12:1, NIV)

Jesus' death was the final sacrifice. But in baptism, we choose to place our own lives on the altar. We die with Christ in the water so we can rise with Him in the Spirit.

"Very truly I tell you, unless a kernel of wheat falls to the ground and dies, it remains only a single seed. But if it dies, it produces many seeds."
(John 12:24, NIV)

This is what it means to be born again.

If you are serious about Christ being Lord of your life, you'll often hear Him say that you need to be baptised. Once you're saved, you must be born again by baptism.

To be baptised is to declare: I am no longer a citizen of this world and its destruction of life, but a citizen of the Kingdom of Heaven, an ambassador for Christ on earth.

"Jesus answered, 'Very truly I tell you, no one can enter the kingdom of God unless they are born of water and the Spirit. Flesh gives birth to flesh, but the Spirit gives birth to spirit.'"
(John 3:5–6, NIV)

This is not just symbolism, it is a command to echo our heart's posture toward Christ. If you want to break away from a life of death, wouldn't you run to a life in Him?

In Acts 8, we see a man receive a revelation of what he must do. **Without delay**, he stops his journey and finds a river to be baptised by a disciple of Jesus.

"As they travelled along the road, they came to some water and the eunuch said, 'Look, here is water. What can stand in the way of my being baptised?' And he gave orders to stop the chariot. Then both Philip and the eunuch went down into the water, and Philip baptised him."
(Acts 8:36–38, NIV)

Chapter 11: The Kingdom Invitation: Coming to Christ, Dying to Self, and Rising in New Life

It is a bold step of surrender, a public declaration of an internal transformation. And a reflection of the heart and soul desire to follow the Word of God.

The Burning Bush, the Living Branches, and the Eternal Flame

In Exodus 3:2, Moses encounters a bush that burns, but is not consumed. This was not just a sign. It was a *prophecy*.

It was a glimpse into what God would do in us.

In Acts 2, fire fell again, this time on the disciples. The fire didn't destroy them; it empowered them. The fire once on the bush is now on the *branches*.

"I am the vine; you are the branches."
(John 15:5, NIV)

We are now that bush. Set ablaze by the Holy Spirit. Still living, yet fully surrendered.

The altar hasn't disappeared, it has moved inside us. The fire still burns and it must never go out.

A Sacred Pause: Yielding to Christ

Right now, I want to make space for those who are ready to yield.

You've heard the call.
You've seen the fire.
You've sensed the invitation.

This Is Love, Not Religion

This isn't about joining a religion.
It's about entering a *relationship*.
It's not about working your way to God.
It's about *surrendering* to the One who already came for you.

If your heart is stirring,
if you sense a pull in your soul,
if you're tired of carrying life on your own strength...

This is your moment to yield.
To return.
To come home.

A Prayer of Salvation

You can pray these words from your heart, wherever you are. Speak them aloud or whisper them within. God hears. He's listening.

Lord Jesus, I come to You.
I admit that I have sinned,
and I cannot save myself.
But I believe that You died for me
and rose again to give me new life.
I confess You now as my Lord and Saviour.
I give You my heart.
I give You my past.
I give You my future.
Wash me clean.
Fill me with Your Holy Spirit.
Make me new.
Help me to walk in Your truth
and rest in Your love.
Today, I choose You.
Thank You for choosing me.
In Your name I pray, Amen

Final Thoughts: Rooted for Life – Becoming the Tree We Were Born to Be

"They will be called oaks of righteousness, a planting of the Lord for the display of his splendour." (Isaiah 61:3, NIV)

You made it. Not just to the end of a book, but to the threshold of a deeper beginning. You are not the same person who turned the first page. Somewhere between the roots, the vine, the fruits and the seasons, you began to grow.

This journey was never just about information. It was about transformation. Speaking of, in order to be here and write this book I asked God to help me be well in all areas of the framework I now teach. I didn't want to be false, or a hypocrite. It's only as I was writing this, I realised that I am able to be here in His fulfilment. It took years but He was working in me before I initially prayed that prayer. And yet, there's still much more work to be done. You see, this journey with the Lord is about becoming more like Him, but even more importantly, it's about simply being... with Him.

You've discovered the God who plants with intention. You've walked through what it means to be rooted in the Seven Spirits of God: The Holy Spirit. You've traced the Vine of Christ, following each pillar of growth: Boundaries; Identity;Animation;Management; Artistry;Purpose and Love. You've begun to see how that connection births visible fruit in every area of life: Godliness; Mindset; Well-being; Family; Community; Work and Wealth. And you've learned that none of it happens all at once, but always in season.

Now, you stand like a tree planted by streams of living water *(Psalm 1)*. Not because life is perfect, but because you've allowed yourself to be planted. Because you chose to stay when it was easier to run. Because you opened your heart to truth when lies were more familiar. Because you dared to believe that you are not only a branch, but part of the whole garden God is restoring.

You Are Becoming the Tree

This isn't the end of your story, it's the turning of soil for the next season. You are becoming the tree you were born to be. Strong in your identity. Flourishing in your design. Fruitful in your season. Each part of you -your mind, your heart, your hands- has something sacred to offer.

Whether you've known God for years or you're just now opening to the possibility of divine love, this journey is for you. The soil doesn't reject the seed, it receives it. And if you've made it this far, then something in you has already taken root.

Final Thoughts: Rooted for Life – Becoming the Tree We Were Born to Be

An Invitation to Remain

Jesus said, *"Remain in me and I also remain in you...apart from me you can do nothing"* (John 15:4–5, NIV)

That's not a warning, it's a comfort. You don't have to bear fruit on your own. You're not meant to.

You are invited to:
- Stay rooted in reverence, where the fear of the Lord keeps you anchored.
- Stay aligned in identity, where truth is your foundation.
- Stay creative in expression, where your animation carries purpose.
- Stay structured in intention, where management orders your world.
- Stay bold in artistry, where your life becomes a masterpiece.
- Stay faithful in pursuit, where purpose fuels every step.
- Stay present in love, where God's Spirit keeps flowing.

For some of us, we want to be all we can be in Christ. But we find ourselves leaning to control things in our own way. Then when life stirs left, we want things back right. Then we call on Him. God is not a backup we run to when it's convenient, only to walk away once we've gotten what we came for. How fortunate are we to be chosen and loved, to be recipients of His grace and mercy, of His patience and plan for our lives.

Stay in the Vine. Keep tending your garden. Water what's good. Prune what needs letting go. Above all, abide in love.

Have Grace for One Another

Growth is personal. And it's messy. It takes time, patience and an extraordinary amount of grace. Remember: no one is righteous on their own. We've all sinned. But in Christ, we have been made righteous, not by effort, but by grace through faith.

When you walk with God, you can't help but see Him do His work of glory in other people's lives. You begin to discern what He has done, and what He has yet to do. Grace isn't just seen in your story; it becomes visible in others too.

His grace is activated by humility. When you are in a humble position, you'll see His hand. But when you've truly humbled yourself, you'll begin to see more of Him. In this walk of faith, you will be tested, not to break you, but to prove your integrity and prepare you for expansion.

Moses is described in Scripture as the most humble man on the face of the earth *(Numbers 12:3)*. And yet, through this very humility, God displayed His power in undeniable ways, through signs, wonders, deliverance, and divine wisdom. Because Moses was empty of self, God could fill him fully. His humility became the vessel through which God's glory was revealed.

There will be moments when you're stretched beyond yourself, and even fall short of His glory. But those who humble themselves will encounter His mercy. His grace becomes a sign, not of your perfection, but of His forgiveness and love. He wants you to succeed, but you need power beyond your own strength. This power is grace: the unmerited favour of God, given so that His glory may be revealed in and through you.

This is why forgiveness is so important. You block true transformation if you are unforgiving. Unforgiveness says you'll be the judge that upholds true rulership. It says you'll take the place of God in your life and in the life of another. How can you leave no room for God and expect change?

To help others change, we must first surrender to God's transforming work in our own lives. That change begins by walking in the opposite direction of our current behaviour and turning towards God, a full 180-degree shift. A repentance. Not just a moment of regret, but a lifelong journey of surrender.

Final Thoughts: Rooted for Life – Becoming the Tree We Were Born to Be

Along the way, you'll discover that true transformation starts with subduing the enemy's devices within you, before ever attempting to address them in someone else. And when it comes to helping others, do so only when permitted. Even Jesus waits at the door and knocks, He never forces His way into someone's heart. If Christ honours boundaries, so should we.

So love people as they are, not as you want them to be. Don't push for change where you haven't first received permission. Honour boundaries. Respect the pace of someone else's process. And most of all, look first to the change that still needs to happen in your own life.

Transformation is the Lord's work. We are invited to plant, water and walk alongside, but only God brings growth.

Love and the Will: Stones in the Wilderness

In the wilderness, Jesus was not without love.
He was full of the Spirit, led by God, not by fear.
But that wilderness also held a voice.
A voice that offered shortcuts.

Not to pleasure, but to power.
Not to sin in the obvious sense,
But to control, compromise, and speed.

Each temptation wasn't just a test of strength.
It was a whisper away from presence.
An invitation to step outside the rhythm of love,
And into the realm of striving.

And this was not the first time a choice like this appeared.

The Stone and the Garden: A Parallel of Wills

This moment echoes Eden.

In Genesis 2, Adam was told not to eat from the Tree of the Knowledge of Good and Evil,
Not because knowledge is evil,
But because taking it apart from God
Was rebellion.

Adam chose his will.
Jesus, in contrast, chose the Father's.

Where Adam reached for more,
Jesus refused to grasp.
Where Adam fell at the tree,
Jesus stood before the stone.

He could have turned it to bread.
He didn't.

He could have thrown Himself down.
He didn't.

Because love doesn't move without the Father.
And love always trusts the presence over the performance.

The wilderness and the garden both ask the same question:
Whose will shapes the stone in your hand?

The Stone as Symbol: Will in Our Hands

"If You are the Son of God, tell this stone to become bread."
(Luke 4:3, NIV)

That stone is more than an object.
It is will, built of the words you live by in your heart.

Final Thoughts: Rooted for Life – Becoming the Tree We Were Born to Be

It represents the quiet beliefs that drive your decisions:
"I must provide for myself."
"I have to prove who I am."
"If I don't act now, I'll miss my chance."

The stone is a choice:
To act from presence or from pressure.
To trust God's rhythm, or chase your own.

Jesus, though hungry, refused to move outside of love.
He didn't act to silence the enemy.
He stayed in step with the Father.

Because love doesn't turn stones into shortcuts.
It turns them into testimonies.

That stone was not just a hazard.
It was the path.
Jesus didn't stumble,
Because He stayed aligned with God's will.

And through Scripture, we see stones used again and again to reveal the same truth.

When Stones Align With God's Will

- **David's five stones** were declarations of faith, not in ambition, but in God. *(1 Samuel 17:40)*
- **Jacob's stone pillow** became a place of dreams and altars. *(Genesis 28:11–18)*
- **God's law** was written on stone, not to bind, but to bless. *(Exodus 31:18)*
- **Jesus' tomb** was sealed with a stone, a final word from the world: "He is dead."
  But that stone rolled away.
  What looked final was only beginning.

This Is Love, Not Religion

Truth always has the last word.

When Stones Defy God's Will

- **Cain lifted a stone**, not to build, but to kill.
  A brother's body broken by the envy of self-will. *(Genesis 4:8)*
- **The Pharisees held stones**, ready to condemn the woman caught in adultery.
  But Jesus invited them to drop what love would never hold. *(John 8:7–9, NIV)*
- **Korah's rebellion** brought death, but God told Moses to collect twelve stones afterward as a sign.
  What began in defiance ended in remembrance. *(Numbers 16–17; Joshua 4:7)*

Every stone speaks.
The question is whose will it's shaped by.

And the temptations of Jesus show us what these choices really look like.

The Real Temptations: Stepping Away from Love

1. **Turn These Stones to Bread** (Lust of the Flesh)
   Satisfy yourself before God satisfies you.
   But love waits on the Word. It does not rush to fill.
2. **Worship Me and I'll Give You Everything** (Lust of the Eyes)
   Shortcut to success without surrender.
   But love wants the Giver, not just the gift.
3. **Throw Yourself Down, He'll Catch You** (Pride of Life)
   Test God to prove He's real.
   But love doesn't demand proof. It trusts the presence.

Final Thoughts: Rooted for Life – Becoming the Tree We Were Born to Be

> These temptations may sound ancient, but their echoes are everywhere in our age.

Application: Love in the Age of Speed

We live in a world of shortcuts.
AI. Influence. Automation.
You can build a brand, write a message, craft a vision,
Without ever consulting heaven.

But when your will overrides God's word,
Even good things become dangerous.

Love teaches us to slow down.
To discern the source of our goals.
To resist the devil's twisted truths, even when they sound like Scripture.
To refuse to compromise identity just to gain visibility.
To wait for bread from heaven,
Even when the stone in your hand feels heavy with potential.

Because love doesn't force fruit.
It flows from rhythm.

And in that rhythm, every stone becomes a testimony of trust.

Let the Stone Speak of Trust

You may be holding a "stone" today:
A calling. A dream. A deadline.
Something you could turn into something else,
But without God's yes.

Don't shape it with insecurity.

This Is Love, Not Religion

Don't throw it in fear.
Don't strike it out of frustration.

Wait.

Because the stone that looked like an end
May just be the beginning of resurrection.

"Submit yourselves, then, to God.
Resist the devil, and he will flee from you."
(James 4:7, NIV)

Victory doesn't come by striving.
It comes by submission.
By staying in the place of love,
Even when it's quiet.
Even when it's dry.
Even when the stone has not yet moved.

Because if love has led you there,
Love will lead you out.

And that's when it hit me,
If even Jesus was tempted to perform for love,
To move ahead of God's voice,
Then no wonder I had spent so much of my life
Mistaking performance for intimacy.

But the stone is not the end. It's the beginning of something greater.

From Stone to Mountain

In the Kingdom, even the smallest thing carries the weight of eternity.
A single stone can change the shape of a river.
A single word from God can alter the course of a life.

Final Thoughts: Rooted for Life – Becoming the Tree We Were Born to Be

A stone is like a word or a will, specific, intentional and placed where it belongs.
It might seem small, but in God's hands, it holds purpose.
In man's hands, it can be used for good or for harm, to build an altar of worship *(Genesis 28:18)* or to cast at another in judgment *(John 8:7)*.
What matters is not just the stone itself, but the spirit in which it is placed.

A rock is what happens when that word is received and believed.
It becomes a foundation, something you can stand on when the winds rise.
Jesus said, "Upon this rock I will build my church, and the gates of hell will not prevail against it" *(Matthew 16:18)*.
David declared, "The Lord is my rock, my fortress and my deliverer" *(Psalm 18:2)*, showing that belief in God becomes both stability and safety.

But a mountain, a mountain is more.
It is the kingdom reality rising in every sphere of life, where God's justice, mercy, and truth flow down like rivers to the valleys below *(Micah 4:1–2)*.
It is the place where heaven's order shapes earth's reality and where nations are drawn to walk in His ways.

Yet mountains are not always holy.
In Scripture, a mountain can also symbolise pride, rebellion, or kingdoms built on human strength.
Some mountains exalt God's glory; others exalt themselves against Him *(Obadiah 1:3–4, Revelation 17:9)*.
Whether a mountain becomes a refuge or a stronghold of resistance depends entirely on its foundation.

This is the journey of growth:
From a single word...
To a life built on belief...

To a mountain that becomes a refuge, a witness, a place of encounter.
And here is the mystery: this pattern is not just in our lives, it is in the Gospel itself.
When Jesus was crucified, they laid His body in a tomb carved out of the rock *(Matthew 27:59–60)*.
A great stone was rolled against the entrance *(Mark 15:46)*, a final seal, meant to close the chapter.
That stone was meant to keep death in and hope out.

But on the third day, the stone was rolled away *(Luke 24:2)*, not to let Jesus out, for death could never hold Him, but to let the world see that the grave was empty.
What began as a single stone sealing the end became the doorway into a new reality.

In that moment, the stone of God's word fulfilled became the rock of our salvation *(Psalm 118:22; Acts 4:11)*.
And from that rock rose the mountain of His Kingdom, a reign without end, drawing every nation to the light of His glory *(Isaiah 2:2–3)*.

The resurrection was more than a victory over death.
It was the rising of the mountain of the Lord, the unveiling of a kingdom that will never be shaken *(Hebrews 12:28)*.

The Bigger Picture

You are part of something larger, a kingdom without end. A story of redemption, hope, justice and beauty. You are not just growing for you. You are growing for your family, your neighbourhood, your generation and for the glory of the One who called you.

When you grow, others are nourished. When you heal, others find courage. When you love well, others remember how to hope.

Final Thoughts: Rooted for Life – Becoming the Tree We Were Born to Be

This is the Kingdom. Not just in heaven, but here on earth, as it is in heaven.

A Final Blessing

May you become like a tree planted by the river, rooted deep in the love of God, branching wide in the grace of Christ and bearing fruit that feeds a weary world.

You were not just made to survive this life. You were made to flourish.

So go forward-not as the seed that once hoped, but as the tree that now lives to give.

Let your life speak of the Garden to come. Let your fruit taste of heaven. Let your love be the proof.

A key to life is
To love others
And accept love from others.

And whilst you live,
Be present
And live fearlessly,
With shameless audacity,
Within the boundaries of love.

And above all,
Learn the truth about the highest love,
So that you may be free
From oppressive thinking,
Doing,
And being.

Wherever you feel trapped,

This Is Love, Not Religion

There's a path to liberation.
Where you feel formless,
There's an image
You have been called to be.
And wherever you feel empty,
There is fulfilment available.

You have to be willing
To let go of who you are
To become free
In who you've been created to be.
And never forget, you are already growing.

Amen.

John 15:6–17, NIV

If you do not remain in me, you are like a branch that is thrown away and withers; such branches are picked up, thrown into the fire and burned. If you remain in me and my words remain in you, ask whatever you wish, and it will be done for you. This is to my Father's glory, that you bear much fruit, showing yourselves to be my disciples.

"As the Father has loved me, so have I loved you. Now remain in my love. If you keep my commands, you will remain in my love, just as I have kept my Father's commands and remain in his love. I have told you this so that my joy may be in you and that your joy may be complete. My command is this: Love each other as I have loved you. Greater love has no one than this: to lay down one's life for one's friends. You are my friends if you do what I command. I no longer call you servants, because a servant does not know his master's business. Instead, I have called you friends, for everything that I learned from my Father I have made known to you. You did not choose me, but I chose you and appointed you so that you might go and bear fruit—fruit that will last—and so that whatever you ask in my name the Father will give you. This is my command: Love each other.
(John 15:6–17, NIV)

About the Author

Aiden Saunders is the founder of *The Ailey* and a Personal Growth Partner who helps people rest in high standards across every area of life. For more than seven years, he has developed and taught a *Framework for Freedom*, a practical, values-driven approach to strengthening boundaries, abiding in true identity, and living with purpose.

Raised in East London, Aiden used the opportunities he had to pursue his passion for sport. A basketball scholarship took him to the United States, where he earned a Business Management degree and won championships. Beyond the court, those years challenged his values, character, and vision for life, shaping the principles he now teaches.

On returning to the UK, Aiden began working with students from primary to university level through basketball coaching. Over time, this work evolved beyond sport into life coaching, equipping people with the mindset, boundaries, and values needed to thrive.

Through *The Ailey*, Aiden's mission is to strengthen human-to-human relationships as the foundation of personal and societal growth, using technology as a tool to serve and enhance those connections. His vision is to set a culture that reflects Kingdom principles, investing in and shaping people, communities, and nations so that a high standard of living is recognised, appreciated, envisioned, and practiced.

This book, **This Is Love, Not Religion**, is an extension of that mission: to help readers slow down, grow deep roots, and live fruitful, whole lives that reflect love in action.

www.ingramcontent.com/pod-product-compliance
Lightning Source LLC
Chambersburg PA
CBHW041306240426
43661CB00011B/1034